Fabio Ghia

Senator Trump Save Ameri*k*a

The Theory of "Permanent Instability":
Political and Social Policy of the US and
Europe in the Mediterranean Area and in the
Middle East

"We do not work hard to create a better future for ourselves or our children, but to create it for our grandchildren."

CONTENTS

Acknowledgements

English translation and editing performed by Mr. David Casani (who successfully accomplished a similar task in the book *International Business Law* published by CEDAM and Wolters Kluwer, in March 2016).

Introduction

During summer 2015, Europe has seen the worst pages of its history from the end of World War II. Tens of thousands immigrants entered into Europe through Hungary, demanding to move to their craved final destination, Germany. Due to the massive migration occurred in 2015, Europe has become aware that migration flows, particularly those of refugees, are not solely a problem of Italy, but they represent a social, economic, and political issue for the European Community as a whole and - perhaps – to the rest of the world.

European politicians and tank-thinkers paid rather little attention to the events that generated this migration flows, while the media focused on the humanitarian tragedy - millions people were uprooted from their homelands and forced to desperately move in other countries. Certainly, the international community is on the side of displaced Syrians, especially when it comes to children, but no one should forget that some international actors, which are hard to identify, caused this artificial crisis. For example, the worldwide dominant American foreign policy and its connections with the energy policy of the Gulf countries marks the origin of the socio-cultural destabilization in the entire Middle East and the Mediterranean area.

Furthermore, both the United States and the European Union failed to stabilize those countries where multiple national actors gave rise to riots, revolutions, and wars that were caused by Islamic fundamentalists who professed a biased and partial religious dogma. Eventually, it is also worth to note that fundamentalism does not represent the Islamic world in its entireness; this is the main reason that explains why so many individuals are fleeing from places like Syria, Libya, Afghanistan, and Iraq.

At the same time, countries that are in total disarray like Somalia, Nigeria, Sudan, Ethiopia, Niger, and Libya cried out in despair in the attempt to grab the attention of a "deaf" European Union that provoked social unrests in these countries due to the application of erroneous foreign policies. For example, Europe abandoned Somalia after the civil war in 1992-1993, and Islamic fundamentalists took control of the country without facing much resistance. As a direct consequence of the inconsistent application of adequate foreign policies, the United States and the European Union have left these countries on their own, without any hope for economic recovery.

The military intervention in Iraq evidently showed the flaws of the American foreign policy. Since that period, President Obama developed the American strategy called "Stay Behind", which was combined with the encouragements given to the Arab partners in the energy sector, to uphold the rebellions in the Middle East.

The new regional power, Saudi Arabia, became the nurturing country of Wahhabism, where Sunnis comfortably professed their primordial faith. Moreover, Saudi Arabia pulled the trigger to start the political-religious revolutions that boomed across the Arab Middle East. After its military occupation and the fall of the dictatorship, Iraq still does not have its own cultural, political, and economic identity; besides, Iraqi citizens keep dying due to terrorists' attacks all over the country and the American mass media hides these facts because it is controlled by the governmental false populist policy of non-interference.

The European Union is partially guilty for the failures in Iraq, too. France and the United Kingdom were enthusiast supporters of the attack on Libya and they pushed other European governments to accept the idea that the regime led by Assad needed to be overthrown. Although Assad used to lead a dictatorship, the European military and economic resources that were unleashed to destroy his administration seemed to be far more powerful and dangerous than his regime. The analysis of the events that occurred seems to be complicated from an economic and political point of view, and it becomes more articulated from the cultural standpoint. In fact, The Mediterranean area has always been a crossroads of civilizations and a melting pot of different cultures that attempted to take over each other. However, cultural integration and all related matters have never been tested so hard in history.

On the one side, there is the Islamic world that yearns for a new political, religious, and social identity, so that it is now subject to a state of internal conflict between Islamic fundamentalism and Modernism. The lack of an identity helped fundamentalists to gain political influence and resources to increase their military power, which they needed to create armed groups like Al Qaeda, ISIS, Al Nosra in Nigeria, and Daëch in Libya. Within this cultural framework, the State and its policies, religion and its dogmas, and "philosophical reasoning" are more often comparing with one another to found better social rules. In particular, the traditional model of society, which emphasizes all aspects of religion and the role of women in the family and society attracts Turkey, Egypt, Tunisia, Lebanon, Algeria, Morocco, and most countries of Northern Africa.

On the other side, the European Mediterranean countries are witnessing rapid social changes. New debates are held every day about unmarried couples, the legalization of homosexual weddings, the growing conviction that the well-being of society is linked to individual well-being, which is exclusively empowered by material certainties and egoistic personal interests. Some European philosophers also suggested that homosexual couples should receive the right to have their children through assisted insemination, but this is a paradox with the Islamic culture.

In practice, European materialism tends to create new life forms and societies whose core values (the highest values have religious backgrounds) are not identifiable with those ones that the three-thousand-plus years have given rise to modern society. In particular, when the new European values and the Islamic dogmas are compared with one another, the former promote opposite and contrasting values against the cultural basis of Islam, and Europe is consequently favoring the widespread of individuals professing Islam.

In spite of their cultural divisions, mass migration is the common factor uniting the two worlds of the West and the Middle East. Tunisia has 1.1 million immigrants more than Europe (12% of the population); however, the different legal and educational systems, and the different cultural values and traditions may create social unrests discouraging integration between European civilizations and Islamic cultures. The assumption offered in this brief introduction is that the perception of life itself is changing for the worse. Philosophers, politicians, and tank-thinkers must analyze, discuss, and find quick solutions to the contrasts that are typical between the Western and the Islamic cultures; if fear for "the Other", social unrest, and hatred continue to spread, Europeans will suffer new horrific events like the attacks at Charlie Hebdo.

Above all, national and international institutions have to promote cultural integration between the European Union and foreign societies, as well as international organizations should not underestimate the consequences of the revolutions that arose in the Southern part of the Mediterranean area. In particular, reciprocal cultural knowledge has become a key factor in the process of understanding "the Other"; therefore, interreligious and intercultural exchanges of information and cultural comparison are, nowadays, the best tools that modern society can use to encourage cultural integration between different civilizations.

The following paper analyzes the political mistakes that have been committed in the most recent years through the examination of events that occurred in the Mediterranean area and in the Middle East, and it provides applicable solutions to improve cultural integration.

Chapter I - The Turmoil in the Mediterranean Area and in the Middle-East

On February 3, 2015, I published the following article on the newspaper *L'Opinione* in order to clarify some aspects of the political and military chaos that shattered Libya into pieces. Here, I wish to propose again the same article because it explains well the state of confusion in which the international framework had operated, especially the European one. Second, the article anticipated the possibility that the terrorist group Daëch in Libya would try to break in Tunisia to undertake some attacks, which eventually occurred in March 2015 at the Bardo Museum (32 victims) and in June in Sousse (37 victims); all victims came from European countries. Few months later, on November 23, a Jihadist blew himself up to kill the highest authorities of the country. At last, the article draws the path to study and critically analyze the complex world of Islam, with particular emphasis on Saudi Arabia.

Libya and "the Other" Islam

Yesterday, Minister Gentiloni, in his urgent parliamentary intervention about the situation in Libya, claimed for "direct action" through the increasing application of "International Communitarian" measures. The latter are a prelude to what the UN Security Council, pressed by President Obama who is the founder of the "Stay Behind" strategy, is evaluating in the coming hours.

Successively, Minister Pinotti was giving assurance that the Italian Armed Forces are ready to take action for a mission in Libya under UN auspices. The Prime Minister Renzi fell in silence, after he tried to put on hold any kind of military occupation and he opposed to armed intervention; in other words, Italy seems to be rather confused and uncertain about what is happening in the Islamic world, particularly in Libya. Besides, many other European nations shows a certain cultural backwardness in their assessments, especially, against Islam.

European governments distinguish criminal organizations like ISIS, Al-Qaeda, Salafis, Al Qaeda Maghreb, and Boko Haram, from all the "nations" of Muslim belief, without realizing that Islam is always the same, indistinct, single dogma. Certainly, some Muslims behave better than others do; therefore, the international community can separate them into "good Islamic" and "evil Islamic" followers. This simple division among Muslims shows that the religious community of the Middle East is internally in turmoil; therefore, the war against fundamentalism should be fought by European countries as well as by "good Muslims". This internal clash of Islamic cultures, which currently affect a minority of the International monotheistic community, is merely the prelude to a vast and more complicated "psychological warfare and war of communication".

This thesis is supported by the fact that the "Arab Spring" countries have come out from the "revolutionary" period and are moving the first steps towards new forms of "Islamic democracy". In spite of these successes, Tunisia heavily spilled the blood of its citizens to earn a Democratic regime. In the last month, 16 civilians were brutally murdered on a bus by Jihadists (Salafi) with Kalashnikovs at Kasserin; then, an officer of the National Guard was assassinated in public in Jandouba. Furthermore, five soldiers were killed in a firefight on the mountains that are close to the border with Algeria; and, yesterday, "Four members of the National Guard" became national heroes as the result of a terrorist attack in Kasserin, which is on the border with Algeria. The main Tunisian jihadist group claimed ownership of the massacre; the terrorist group is known by the name "Uqba ibn Nafi", which is linked to Al-Qaeda Maghreb, and it operates in the mountainous border between Algeria and Tunisia.

In the meanwhile, Tunisian security forces continue to practice "counterterrorism operations" or precautionary arrests of Taksiri (Salafis "inspectors" who have the power to murder those individuals who do not fully respect the Sharia!) and Jihadist suspects. In short, the actions preventing Islamic terrorism are producing every-day victims since Ben Alì reached power. In Tunisia, the official army is a plethora of Jihadist groups which, fortunately, still lack coordination. Additionally, Egypt is another post-revolutionary nation; but radicals like Morsi and General Al Sisi governed the country after the revolution. Morsi is currently in jail under tight surveillance, but the Salafist Muslim Brothers continue to spill blood in order to re-establish the ancient Caliphate.

15

The situation is extremely dangerous in Libya, where the Premier Abdallah Al Thani confirmed that members of Boko Haram and ISIS have joined forces with the main terrorist groups operating in Libya. The naïve Western world hope to achieve a possible reconciliation of the Libyan factions, insisting on the institutionalization of social, political, and tribal dialogue. However, the reality is quite different.

Under the auspices of Qatar (USA and Saudi Arabia, too) and Turkey, the toughest international jihadism has emerged in Syria and Iraq, and many other terrorist groups are growing. The revolution of February 17, 2011, which dismantled the authoritarian regime of Muammar El Gaddafi, has completely deviated from its course and objectives to militarize society and the various national, local, and tribal institutions, with the authorization of the Special Commissioner of the United Nations.

Today, in Libya, there are more than three armies: the "regular" army headed by General Al Haftar that is as weak as the old regime; the second group is formed by members of ISIS; and, a third army know by the name "Fajr Libya" that operates under the command and governance of the Islamists who live in Tripoli. In addition, there is a plethora of other small groups controlled by "Ansar Echariaâ", and Daëch attracts multiple local tribes with its jihadist populism.

The UN, Western governments, and the international community monitored the situation without taking actions, in the last two years, so the number of Islamic fundamentalists increased under the command of Ansar Echariaâ, which united different jihadist forces in Derna and Misrata. Day by day, due to the negligence of European institutions, these groups have come together under the black flag of the Caliphate in the attempt to conquer Tripoli, and they are now pressing on the borders of Tunisia. The Ansar Echariaâ's group is certainly the most powerful in Libya because it has many soldiers, good armaments, and a well-structured internal organization. Last year, the group of Al Haftar has lost several strategic areas like Tripoli, and it will soon collapse in Benghazi, too, where the jihadists of Daëch are regularly increasing their military presence.

Definitively, due to the application of erroneous foreign policies promoted by the French President Sarkozi and Bernard Henry Levy, Libya has become the dreamland of Jihadists for the reason that a functional state no longer exists in this country! Unfortunately, Somalia suffered the same fate many years ago; and,

16

there too, the shady hand of the American government was highly involved in that matter!

Therefore, the Jihadists linked to Al-Qaeda (Ansar Echariaâ) and Daëch have a clear-cut advantage on the naive and "surreal plans" of the UN special envoy (France), which continue to pursue a failing solution based on the peaceful demilitarization of the jihadist militias like Daëch, in spite of all warnings and negative feedback from the International community. In the meanwhile, taking into account the heavy Egyptian air strike, and the beheading of 21 Christians citizens (Copts), the international community should get ready to receive news about ISIS that will most probably move towards the western border of Tunisia.

Tunisia, which does not have many choices because it has neither an army of two million men like Egypt nor strategic and energy interests to trade, will have to remain extremely vigilant to do not fall into the quicksand of an unpredictable future. In the next few days, if Daëch moves to Tunisia and temporarily withdraws from the Egyptian border, in spite of every proclamation against Italy and the Christians, it will provoke random and heavy damages in Northern Africa, with particular focus on Tunisia!

Eventually, the "Caliph" Al-Baghdadi may take advantage of the current political and military situation in Libya, which will be invaded by "European crusaders" and "corrupted apostates" (Egyptians, Jordanians, and other Arabs and Africans). In light of these observations, I am convinced that the UN Security Council will vote in favour of a "non-intervention" action and the continuation of diplomacy; however, the USA will surely take the lead of diplomatic relations in order to preserve its energy interests in the Mediterranean area, as it devastatingly did in the Middle East.

What should European countries do? First, they must not fall into the trap of a military intervention in Muslim countries as well as they must not open new war fronts that are impossible to win. In fact, fundamentalists are just waiting to declare a defensive war against the "Western oppressors", (Christian and apostates) if the latter decide to perform a military invasion. Second, national and international institutions have to use all the diplomatic tools available to convince the United States, the Saudis, and Qatar to cut permanently the flows of money going to armed groups; the actors involved in this matter must have a strong will to stop terrorist groups, while supporting Europe and the modernist Arabic world. Third, the international community should provide humanitarian aid to the Libyan population who is suffering the consequences of these

17

conflicts, and try to redistribute the more than 2 million Libyans who are living in Tunisia, so to increase the number of transit visas towards secure destinations that are far away from any conflict.

Last, but not least important, some international organizations have to offer their full support to Southern Mediterranean countries demanding cultural support, like Tunisia. At the same time, other organizations should provide logistical support (transportation, helicopters) and military advisers to the Governmental Armed Forces, including new leadership, which will be given the duty to "contain" the conflict in Libya. Looking at the current military situation in Libya, the Governmental Armed Forces are just the second most reliable institution of the country, behind the Caliphate.

I always hope that one of the Gods belonging to the three monotheistic religions will protect the world in peace, and it will not encourage humanity to declare new wars in the name of "submission", as it is written in the Koran (do not forget!).

In this article, I also wrote that Mrs. Deborah K. Jones was appointed as UN representative in Libya, and she replaced Mr. Chris Stevens who was brutally killed in September 2012 in Benghazi. The US expected great achievements from her, but she failed expectations. Once again, in fact, the Obama's strategy relied on the axis with Saudi Arabia and Qatar, leaving in the hands of the Libyan Islamists the opportunity to reopen the dialogue with the modernist part of the parliament in Benghazi, which owned the political and territorial majority of the country.

Additionally, the original article provides an in-depth analysis of three main topics, including 1) the comparison between Libya and Somalia after Siad Barre, and the invisible hand of the USA in the political scenario; 2) the change of the strategy adopted by the USA; and, 3) the description of the main actors who fight each other in the Islamic world to earn the future "Governance".

Chapter II – The Case of Somalia

On December 22, 1992, four hundred men belonging to the Ship *San Giorgio* landed together with troops carried by helicopters, and, in just more than three hours, they took possession of the old port of Mogadishu so to build the necessary structures to receive reinforces. Through this military task, Italian soldiers moved their first steps in Mogadishu, and they engaged in a "peacekeeping operation" under the auspices of the United Nations; then, they joined forces together with an army composed by other four hundred men who explored the area of the airport from December 16. The mission was accomplished without victims, because the entire area had been "sanitized" 24 hours before the arrival of the troops by Italian operatives belonging to the *San Marco* regiment along with members of the SISMI.

The mission of "humanitarian intervention" assigned to the naval forces had been perceived by most local citizens as a peaceful action to support the population, in spite of the fact that the reputation of Italians in Somalia fell drastically after the removal of Siad Barre (due to the improper use of funds given by the "International cooperation" program). In particular, many Italian soldiers who used to live in the city informed the local population about the arrival of new troops.

The objective given to American land troops and to the Italian *Folgore* was quite different, as they had to "demilitarize" all Somali forces (seven factions!) and prepare the way for their peace talking and diplomatic negotiations. The blue helmets belonging to the International Forces were 25000, while the bulk of the Somali fighters guided by Aideed and Ali Mahdi (the main leaders) were about 15000. Additionally, the latter could receive full support from the local population, and this important clue should not be underestimated.

Since December 15, the green line divided the city into three main zones, where the armed soldiers of the international coalition established some checkpoints (remember the checkpoint "pasta"!) to maintain control and proceed with the pacification of the territory. However, the unsuccessful "Operation Restore Hope" marked the failure of the mission and the abandonment of Somalia to the rebel forces of Aidid and Ali Mahdi, who were joined by the jihadists of "Al Shabaab".

Although the United Nations only approved missions of "humanitarian intervention", the United States justified the "use of force" to contrast the brutal behavior of the militias belonging to the Somali warlords, so American Generals gave the order to maintain the control over the territory at all costs, and soldiers used all possible means to respect this order.

Initially, humanitarian initiatives in Somalia were possible only because the UN troops could secure the key areas of the country and restore civil life; furthermore, military deployments to ensure the safety of medical operators and the population supported these initiatives. The Italian ship *San Giorgio* gave its contribution to these initiatives by opening two "medical camps" and multiple food distribution centers in the most remote places on the entire Somali coast. In particular, the UN carefully monitored the situation in Baidoa, which received supplies during a landing mission executed in extreme conditions. The intervention in Somalia was originally planned for the distribution of food, medical supplies including a vaccination plan for children, and the creation of social structures to support the population who mostly used to live in emergency tents and poverty.

The US expressly required the disarmament of the warring factions claiming that they obtained the necessary funds to buy their weaponry from drug trade, and the trafficking of toxic waste that was illegally dumped under the ground and in the sea. When the "humanitarian" objective of the peacekeeping operation became a peace-making mission involving offensive military action, the warring factions widely opposed against the peacemakers by striking direct attacks to UN forces, which were often outnumbered during firefights.

The peace-making mission proved unable to stop the fighting between factions, which actually increased due to the presence of the American army in Somalia. Additionally, from the humanitarian point of view, the US troops reached too late the most sensible areas of the country, and many communities starved to death. The situation got worse in Baidoa, the epicenter of the famine, because the population kicked out the American soldiers from the city. Due to this unfortunate event, the distribution of supplies happened only when the clashing tribes would stop fighting each other for some days. The Italian soldiers of the regiment *San Marco* succeeded in bringing the supplies to the needy population, without intimidating or frightening the local tribes. Other reasons pushed the US to change completely their approach in these areas, including the following:

- After the intervention of the UN in Somalia, the conditions of life became exasperated; the already starving population was force to take refuge in shabby cities made of tents that only the Red Cross could reach in desperate situations. The number of victims suddenly rose because these "cities" were overcrowded and new contagious diseases began to spread around. Four months after the beginning of the operations in Somalia, the overall mortality rate was almost doubled, and the mortality rate of children under five years old quadruplicated.

- The international armed forces proved themselves not particularly suitable to perform security duties to ensure the validity of humanitarian interventions due to their lack of training and ability to use weapons. Besides, just after a month of military intervention, the US decided to double the number of soldiers on the entire Somali territory to maintain international peace and security.

- Eventually, the American population gave a discouraging negative feedback on the military intervention in Somalia. The media put the so-called "warlords" too much under the spotlight; for example, the CNN broadcasted the meeting between Aidid and Ali Mahdi in December 1992.

Furthermore, the Department of State excessively used its men and resources to hunt down Aidid, because the American government had to show its power on the international stage. Kept in check by a general who had to employ a few thousand militiamen, the Marines ended up bogged down in the civil conflict, and they committed unnecessary massacres of unarmed women and children; because of these Western failures, the alienated population became an easy prey for the warlords. Successively, Aidid became a sort of national hero, although the majority of the Somalis would define him as a criminal and an executor of brutal atrocities who will do anything to defend his trade in arms and "chat" (an herbal drug imported from Eritrea and Kenya). Eventually, a violent xenophobic movement against Western "white" invaders broke out in Somalia, and the spirit of the initiative of the international community was demolished.

- In the battle of Mogadishu (October 3, 1993), Somali rebels shot down two "Black Hawk" helicopters; the attack provoked 18 victims and 70 people were wounded among the US Special Forces, and 200 Somali civilians were wounded, too. Pressed by the American public opinion, President Clinton announced the withdrawal of all troops from the country.

The application of erroneous American foreign policies in Somalia triggered a series of new meetings aiming to set up new rules for peacekeeping and peace-making operations. In February 1994, the UN Security Council established that interventions could only involve the protection of ports, airports, and other transportation routes, all of which quickly returned under the control of Somali "warlords".

Chapter III – Leading From Behind. The New American 'World Order'

The disastrous American intervention in Somalia had catastrophic consequences on the adoption of UN "peacekeeping" and peace-making missions; in fact, the US officially announced their new strategy of "non-interference" in the internal affairs of individual states. This decision smoothed the path for the application of the "Leading From Behind" policy (LFB), which is the continuation of the "permanent instability" strategy that debuted in the Oval Office in 1978, under Carter's administration.

In the years following the failure of Somalia, the US consolidated its alliance with Saudi Arabia in the energy sector, and it left out European partners from any agreement; additionally, the nineties promoted the globalization of markets, resulting in the skyrocketing of worldwide energy consumptions. Only a well-orchestrated energy policy between the Americans and the Saudis could counteract the rise in oil prices per barrel, which eventually occurred in 2008. Because of the US economic crisis, the financial speculation on hedge funds and investment funds, and the simultaneous economic liberalization imposed by Saudi Arabia to face the increasing demand of supplies from China, the price of crude oil jumped to 126 US dollars a barrel.

During the first Gulf War, President George H. W. Bush opened diplomatic dialogues with Saudi Arabia, which became the American privileged partner in energy resources, and he led a coalition of 34 nations in the war against Saddam Hussein to liberate Kuwait from the oppression of Iraq. However, the events that occurred in Afghanistan after the withdrawal of the Soviet invaders and the constitution of the *Islamic Republic of Afghanistan* were emblematic.

In 1980, President Reagan supported the Afghan mujahidin and he delivered tactical support and humanitarian aids. Then, since 1996, the US began to provide financial support and training to the mujahidin Pashtuns (as it used to take place under the administration Carter in 1981), which were guided by Mullah Mohammed Omar who was the leader of the Islamic "Taliban" students' movement.

American weapons and Saudi Arabian financial resources transformed the Taliban rebels into an army, which conquered Kabul on September 27, 1996. Today, the international community is well aware of the Taliban behaviors towards the Western world, as well as Western governments identify the connections among the Saudi Osama Bin Laden, the Taliban army, Mullah Omar, the petro-funds received from the Saudi Bin Laden family, several different Saudi sponsors, and the terrorist group of Al Qaeda.

In this period, Saudi Arabia revealed the duplicity of its international policies. On the one hand, it officially got closer with the Western culture and the US through the recognition of international agreements regarding energy supplies. On the other hand, it secretly operated to support the Jihad with funds and other resources, and it sympathized for Al Qaeda. Furthermore, up to the end of the 1990's, the US and the CIA naïvely continued to give technical support to the Taliban rebels in Afghanistan, while Bin Laden was working to "globalize" the strategy of international terror of Al Qaeda with the consent of Mullah Omar.

It is precisely in this period that emerged the dark side of the LFB strategy, in which UN members moved away from the traditional "guardians of the world" approach to adopt strategies of regional warfare and make use of local factions to wage wars. The US was aiming, in particular, to destabilize areas that were already unsafe on their own, so to avoid the intervention of other great powers such as Russia, Iran, and China. In detail, the US relied on Saudi Arabian partners and the Islamic Wahhabi proselytism (we will see later the deep darkness of this definition!), even though it knew that Al Qaeda and the Taliban army could have a chance to bring a destructive wave of chaos in the international environment.

Eventually, the US craved to maintain its leadership in the field of worldwide energy supplies, *in which the Islamic religious ideology had to work as the destabilizing element.* Yet, the US never took into account the fact that fundamentalism, conceived as the antithesis of Western cultures, aims to destroy modern Islam because the latter promotes traditions and values that are typical of the West.

Chapter IV – The Chaos Theory

Zbigniew Brzezinski is a Polish political philosopher, a politician in the US, and the founder of the "permanent instability" strategy pursued by the US for the past thirty years in the international environment. He worked as a National Security Advisor under Carter's administration until 1981, too. He always has been a strategic advisor of the White House, and only President Clinton did not include him in his entourage.

In his biography, Brzezinski writes that he still is a full member of the *Trilateral Commission,* which is composed of more than 300 technocrats who are divided into "Europeans, North Americans, and Asians Pacific." As the Canadian sociologist Gilbert Larochelle asserts in one of his writings "[these three groups constitute] a protected place where the technocracy is law and where sentries, the guard towers, watch and monitor every situation.

Using one's own intellect is not a luxury, and it actually offers the possibility for a civil society to face its problems. *The greater well-being comes only from the mind of the best individuals who, in their inspired superiority, develop new criteria and share them with others.* At last, as a worthy note that needs to be mentioned, Senator Mario Monti was President of the European Group in 2010.

All the sentences written in italics above brings to mind two historical characters: Benjamin Franklin and Ibn Rushd. The first was one of the founding fathers of America, a proponent of a class of elected Americans (all masons!), And a key figure in defining the American ethos. The second was better known as Avorroè, a Muslim philosopher and founder of the "active intellect" deriving from *universal knowledge* that is a dominant feature of philosophers, who are the guardians of the truth on earth.

Moving back to the Trilateral Commission and taking into account the example of Mario Monti as head of the technical government (2011-13) including his miserable results in both the economy and welfare, these groups of "elected" minds has given rise to the infamous *"New World Order."* Once, Mario Monti also stated

> "The technological era will give governments a better chance to control societies. Elites, alien to traditional values, will dominate societies. Every citizen will be subject to continuous surveillance, a great database recording every citizen will be created, and it will be managed by the ruling elite."

However, Brzezinski does not refer to the US controlled centers ("Datagate" - CIA), but to an elite group of people. According to him, real power lies within exclusive political, economic, and military circles, and in the White House. Was Brzezinski pointing the finger towards the Trilateral?

Brzezinski was the mastermind behind the "global chaos" strategy put in place by the US security agency - CIA in 1979, which secretly gave funds to the mujahedeen in Pakistan and Afghanistan in order to free Afghanistan from the Russians, avoiding that the Soviet threat could spread all over Central Asia. In order to carry out the war in Afghanistan, the US commissioned the conflict to the Taliban, who largely received funds from Saudi Arabia.

The Americans trained and armed the Mujahedeen to fight the Soviet-Afghan war, which was the first version of the "proxy war" strategy. The United States cooperated with Pakistan and Saudi Arabia to spread chaos in Afghanistan, and they all strategically destabilized the region in conflict so that the Soviet Union had to intervene. Besides, the Cold War augmented the effects of the "proxy war". The Soviet fiasco in Afghanistan caused great military and economic changes in the international environment, and the balance of powers shifted in favor of the US.

The "proxy war" strategy, therefore, caused so much excitement in the US that it was credited as one of the main factors contributing to the dissolution of the Soviet Union in 1991. As a direct consequence of these events, the US earned the exclusive domination of the world, and they gained great power over global economy and finance. The US had reclaimed its welfare, its strong will, and the undisputed ability to show its military, economic, and diplomatic power to the rest of the world.

Hence, Brzezinski also claimed that

"Euro-Asia is the center of the world economy; therefore, whoever wants to dominate the world must be able to control the vast territory stretching from the Himalayas to Eastern Europe, passing through the Middle East and the Black Sea. It is not a coincidence that the most devastating wars, revolutions, political unrests and terrorist attacks of the past thirty-five years have mostly occurred in that area." - (The Brzezinski Eurasia).

Within this political, military, and economic scenario, the US largely contributed to the implementation of "regional" policies to support the new regional powers like Saudi Arabia and Qatar, which always choked the thirst for power of Russia.

Why Russia was perceived as a danger in the international framework, but China was not? According to Brzezinski, China is an Asian power running a capitalistic economy, while Russia is a Euro-Asian power still capable of influencing European policy and culture. Besides, as the author states that China will become a "buffer State" between Europe and Putin's Russia because the first owns an immense territory that is extremely rich of raw materials (but not oil!), and it is an important economic actor in the European economy.

In order to benefit from this situation, the US will have to reach a compromise with the Chinese government on current domestic policy issues including the recognition of human rights, and the Chinese claim on armaments. Therefore, to sum up the whole theory described in this chapter, Brzezinski promotes the integration of the dominant Chinese authorities within the ruling elite of the Western powers, because he firmly believes that the world does not need the G7 or the G20, but only and solely a "G2 plus" group composed by the duo North America – Euro-Asia.

His strategy, conceived by the end of the 1970's, slyly continued to work through the activity of the State Department until

1996. Successively, under the Clinton administration in 1998, this plan was abruptly halted due to the terrorist attacks on the US Embassies in Dar es Salaam (Tanzania), and Nairobi (Kenya), which were reclaimed by the nascent Al Qaeda of Osama Bin Laden. From this moment onward, the US suspended every support to the Taliban and the CIA began its worldwide hunt on Osama Bin Laden.

Despite its apparent good will to re-establish greater accountability policies of individual actors at the international level, Clinton's administration did nothing against Saudi Arabia, which actually was the financial and ideological sponsor of Al Qaeda. Brzezinski defended Clinton, in 1997, with his new geostrategic theories offered in the book "The Great Chessboard", in which he identifies the American priorities in Eurasia and he explains how they can be implemented in the shortest time. He claimed that the US had to dominate over Eurasia, and that the best way to achieve such goal was to prevent a clash between Russia and China. Unfortunately, the author did not foresee the calamities that Al Qaeda would bring directly on the US.

After the attacks of 09/11, G. W. Bush re-applied the "Pre-emptive war" strategy implemented against Saddam Hussein in Iraq, although the President of the US agreed on having a common energy policy with Saudi Arabia. The same "Pre-emptive war" strategy model was used later against the Talibans in Afghanistan. Furthermore, in these years, new inconsistencies, falsehoods, and misinformation in the American security policy confirmed the return of the LFB strategy.

In 2008, when the international community perceived the American and British desire to wage war against Iraq, President G. W. Bush claimed that he had "evidence" showing the presence of mass-destruction weapons. Europe believed in the Secretary of State Powell and in the British Prime Minister Tony Blair, who pressed for a massive intervention against Saddam. The US and England invaded Iraq, but UN authorities never found the slightest evidence of weapons of mass destruction.

In the case of the Bosnian war, the Western powers announced their military intervention when Serb mortars fired on the civil population in the Muslim market of Sarajevo. However, NATO and English radars determined that the area from which shots were fired was actually under the control of Bosnian Muslim units; therefore, Serbian troops were not involved in the incident. In this period, Saudi Arabia clearly forced the US to intervene in defense of Islamic Bosnians; then, NATO and its allied bombed the area to justify their intervention, and the Russian reaction was immediate. The Kremlin began to modernize its military industry in order to face a possible US / NATO attack against Russia itself.

In the last case of Kosovo, the US tried to blame the Serb forces for the massacres suffered by the population. Although the US media fed the American society with bad news, the raucous provoked by the war did not catch the attention of the American public opinion; therefore, the conflict ended in a short time.

Chapter V – Islamic Orthodoxy

Since 2008, when President Obama entered in the White House, the American international policy has changed. In July, Obama gave a speech in front of two hundred thousand people gathered at the Brandenburg Gate in Berlin, and he said

> "Partnership and cooperation among nations is not a choice; they are the only way to protect everyone's security and humanity. This is the reason why the greatest danger of all is to allow new walls to divide us from each other. The walls between old allies on both sides of the Atlantic cannot stand. The walls between the countries who have more and those who have the least cannot stand. The walls between races and tribes, natives and immigrants, Christians, Muslims and Jews cannot stand. We must tear down these walls."

In this occasion, Obama directly spoke to the main actors of the Mediterranean area, because there is an ideological wall that sharply separates the North Mediterranean cultures from the South Mediterranean ones. According to the unforgettable Oriana Fallaci, this wall expands the wound between the Islamic and the Western cultures, too (September 11, the attacks in London, Madrid, and in the suburbs of Paris) due to the massive immigration of Muslims into Europe.

> "Those riots were and are weapons, another face of this war. They belong to the invasion strategy. A very clever strategy favoring modern Islamic expansionism, which does not need the armies and fleets used by the ancient Ottoman Empire. In reality, fundamentalists just need to 'fuel' the mass migration of immigrants who arrive each day in Sicily, and to whom our own traitors open the doors at the borders, so to let them set on fire our cities. This smart strategy does not imply the use of intimidations, fleets, scimitars, and other barbarities, but it requires preparations, patience, and a continuous pool of new individuals who are ready to die, like the immigrants of the 1st, 2nd, and 3rd generations. For instance, The British bombers of July 7 belonged to the second and third generation; and, the last fall, the French rioters belonged to the second, third, and fourth generation."

Although her analysis about the issues associated to the effective Muslim integration in Europe was correct, Mrs. Fallaci missed some key clues that the Arab Revolutions, still in progress, have just highlighted. The press renamed these revolutions in several different ways like "jasmine", "bread", or "dignity" revolutions; yet, in reality, Arabs were fighting to gain their own social, political, and economic "identity".

The creation of Al Qaeda awoke the political-religious ideology of Wahhabism, which - since 1700 (date of its origin) - had given hope to the entire *Umma* (the whole set of Islamic followers) to profess its original religious Islamic faith. However, fundamentalism from Saudi Arabia spreads rapidly and everywhere, involving mainly the people belonging to low social classes.

In the last century, movements such as the Muslim Brotherhood in Egypt, Tunisian Salafists, the Erdogan's Islamists in Turkey, and the Sunni opposition in Syria, Lebanon, and Iraq increased their supporters, day by day, among the poorest and least educated social classes. Among other things, many social factors increase the dangers of this situation, like marginalization, lack of adequate education, and voluntary ghettoization.

European Muslim immigrants, especially those of second and third generation who did not well integrate in the culture of the countries that gave them hospitality, find their "identity" in Wahhabism, which promotes the pillar values of Islam. However, fundamentalists modify the meanings of these values, so they create an aberrant and perverse interpretation of the Koran, which has given rise to Jihadism and terrorism in the name of an ancient and uncontaminated Islam that existed only in 610-632 AD.

The return to the original Islamic social values has caused the emergence of terrorist groups in Europe who gave rise to rebellions and protests in defense of their newfound "identity". Additionally, the Islamic world has entered in contrast with itself, so Muslim "modernists" fight against the religious-political "Orthodoxy" that is typical for the Sunnis in Saudi Arabia, and for the Shiites in Iran.

Brzezinski foresaw the raising contradictions within the Islamic culture, so he thought to exploit this weakness of Islam to give an advantage to the US policy in the international environment. Furthermore, the Iranian Shiite and the Sunni from Saudi Arabia (Ali, was the son of the Prophet Mohamed, the fourth Caliph of Islam, and he created the schism in 656 AD.) engaged each other in a war in Yemen that is better known as "the 30 years conflict". This war generated more social malcontent in those Islamic nations where the modernist reformers were already a minority of the population.

In June 2009, President Obama gave a speech in Cairo, under the wise guidance of Brzezinski, and he opened a new diplomatic dialogue with the Islamic world. Therefore, he claimed that the United States would have diminished their presence in the entire Middle East and Mediterranean regions to increase cooperation with "regional powers", which were culturally closer to the local populations.

In this case, Obama seemed to have forgotten that the US supported the Islamic ideology of some fundamentalists (Bin-Laden), in the earlier decade. Furthermore, this strategy did not achieve greater integration among Islamic and European societies because foreign policies must take into account the "intercultural dialogue" among different cultures who should mutually know, study, and respect each other so to promote a harmonious and peaceful coexistence. Additionally, this event proved that the American government still prefers to cooperate with the Sunni from Saudi Arabia, rather than being more involved with the Iranian Shiite, despite the CIA showed ample evidence of Al Qaeda's deceptive behaviors towards the US policy in the region.

Moreover, President Obama is not the only governmental authority who cooperated with the Arab Sunni to solve issues involving local identities and geographical locations. After WWI, Great Britain, France, and the United States looked at the Middle Eastern countries as potential allies in global politics and economy, although the Sykes-Picot agreement (1916, fall of the Ottoman empire, and formation of new spheres of influence) and the Sevres Treaty (1920, declaration of future independence for Arab countries) had not identified the new international actors, yet. In practice,

England and France wished to maintain their economic power and political influence in the international environment.

While the Arab countries were achieving their independence, two other major events occurred in the same area. First, the last Sultan of the Ottoman dynasty joined forces with the followers of the Ataturk nationalist party and, together, they demanded the expulsion of the Kurds and Armenians through the application of the Sevres Treaty. This request caused the dramatic exodus of one million Greeks who used to live in Asia, and the annexation of Armenian and Kurdish territories to Turkey (History of modern and Contemporary Mediterranean - F. Channel, 330). Second, the USA completely separated Saudi Arabia from the areas of influence assigned to England, and the international community unofficially recognized the new Middle-Eastern state as an independent country. Note that Saudi Arabia was the first country in the Middle East to achieve its full and official independence, in 1927.

If, after WWI, the Western world believed that the Orthodox Islam typical of Saudi Arabia would become a political and economic ally, then WWII eventually confirmed this vision. Think, for instance, to the advent of the State of Israel, the disappearance of the old territories implemented by Jordan, and the beginning of the Palestinian diaspora. In 1950, two years after the recognition of Israel, one million Palestinians fled mainly to Jordan, Lebanon, and Syria. However, today, the UNRWA (UN agency monitoring the movements of Palestinian refugees) claims that more than five million refugees (due to natural population growth) cannot live in their birthplace and acquire a new citizenship in the Arab countries.

A couple of reasons can explain this nonsense; first, Israel refused to implement a resolution of the United Nations on the "Right of Return", because it had the hegemony on the territories of the West Bank. Second, hosting nations claimed that the Palestinians manifested excessive cultural differences. Although, long time ago, there used to be an 80% Christians among the populations, the current situation shows that an overwhelming majority of the Palestinians is Muslim. In fact, Saudi Arabia and the Arab League have always imposed discriminating rules on the acquisition of citizenship in Islamic States, which only Muslims can obtain. In spite of these facts, nowadays, the greatest majority of Islam (Saudi Arabia, the Gulf States, Iran, Pakistan, and others.) has eliminated all discriminating laws, but the Palestinians do not find a permanent solution to this problem.

The above analysis demonstrates that the "acculturation" of the Arab world highly increased the rise of several different political and social Islamic institutions and organizations, which mostly developed their interests and activities in the most "modernist" countries. Usually, these Islamic "forces" are made of peaceful Muslims who look at the Declaration of Human Rights (1948) with great and genuine interest, because they conceive the document as the main source of inspiration to promote a new Constitution, new standards of living, and new models of Democracy.

On the one hand, Tunisia fairly achieved these goals and it gave ample proof of its good will to "modernize" the country; therefore, in 2015, it earned the Nobel Prize for Peace. This award was delivered to the "Quartet" (Unions, Industrial Union, Judiciary Order, and Order of Lawyers) for their ability to open a diplomatic "dialogue" with the Islamist forces of the Government, and for the foundation of the Constitution on behalf of the Tunisian Civil Society! On the other hand, since the fall of the dictator Ben Ali, the financial resources favoring the "modernization" of Tunisia came from Qatar only, and funds were given to the Tunisian government if Saudi Arabia and the US would coordinate their policies without stepping on each other's economic interests.

The greatest proof of how damaging and misleading is the "proxy war" strategy adopted by Obama in recent years lies in the fact that the American President totally missed to foresee the rise of the new social forces within those societies that were subject to post conflict "re-orientation" and "re-organization".

The consequences of the speech delivered in Cairo showed themselves in the Mediterranean area, particularly in those nations that responded to the wicked return of the "proxy wars", through which Wahhabi proselytism widely expanded its range of action.

Fortunately, the events occurring in the last few months are showing that the vast majority of Muslims can understand that, in this world, there is a civil society whose needs have little to do with the spiritual activities imposed by their religious faith. Therefore, although the Western world nominated Saudi Arabia as its "Proxy State" in the Middle East, the new regional power miserably failed in its task of managing the delicate transition to Islamic democracy in the entire area. In practice, Saudi Arabia could not carry out this task because it did not have the right institutional tools to do it, and because the local population was more "educated" and "mature" (harder to manipulate) than expected by both the West and Saudi Arabia.

Above all, taking into account the ideological gap between the Sunni Saudi Arabia and the Shiite Iran, the state of global chaos generated by the American "Leading From Behind – LFB" strategy proved itself to be a double-edged sword that could threaten and hurt Saudi Arabia, and many other countries. For instance, during the war in Yemen, Al Qaeda officially supported and protected the Sunni against the Shiite Houthi in Teheran, but Saudi Arabia got weaker and ideologically more isolated from its Sunni allies (Egypt, Jordan, UAE, Qatar), who managed to set up a "multinational force".

For Saudi Arabia, the situation in Yemen is as much complicated as the Syrian conflict for the Americans; in fact, Russian intervention in Syria has changed the "balance of powers" that were established by the duo Arabia/Qatar (and initially ISIS) since last September. As another relevant factor that must be taken into consideration, Russia is a very important partner in the field of energy resources with Iran, and it used to be a key ally with Assad in Syria, because he allowed them to use a harbor. Furthermore, Iran has sponsored the intervention of the Lebanese Hezbollah to support Assad. No one can exclude, therefore, the hypothesis of an Iranian diplomatic intervention is Syria, which is far more dangerous than the sword printed on the flag of Saudi Arabia.

Chapter VI – The Arab Spring in Tunisia

In 2010-2011, journalists often used the term *Arab Spring* to gather the set of social revolutions that exploded in the Arab states. Tunisia, Libya, Egypt, Syria, Yemen, Algeria, Iraq, Bahrain, Jordan and Djibouti suffered the strongest waves of the revolution, while minor unrests occurred in Mauritania, Saudi Arabia, Oman, Sudan, Somalia, Morocco and Kuwait. On December 17, 2010, in Sidi Bouzid, Mohamed Bouazizi set himself on fire to protest against the dictatorial regime of Ben Ali; the episode triggered a series of social unrests in Tunisia, and the youngest Tunisian generations led the revolt against the local government.

Other factors, though, favored the formation of new outbreaks; the unemployment rate was 50% (higher in the southern part of the country); plus, the lowest social classes lived in misery and poverty, without dignity; and, graduates could not find adequately paid job opportunities. As a direct consequence of these problems, angry students and teachers joined forces together on the social media to protest against the regime, so they prepared the insurrection via Facebook.

Successively, the "Revolution of Dignity" exploded in Tunis, Gafsa, Jandouba, Kairouan, and in many other Tunisian cities. The regime quickly responded with the use of force; in Kasserine, a police group (sent directly from Tunis) opened fire the furious crowed of protesters to scatter it. However, some police officers removed their uniforms, threw away their weapons, and joined the revolt at the sight of blood spilled by civilians. Additionally, violent riots blew up in many other cities, so groups of troublemakers burnt and destroyed unguarded and empty institutional buildings. On January 14, 2011, the regime of Ben Ali collapsed, and his security services escorted him to the airport with his family, too.

The initial impulse of the rebellion, the great participation of young generations, the power of street demonstrations and non-violent protests, which characterized the best moments of these revolutionary movements, did not last very long. In a matter of weeks, every fight turned into a struggle for supremacy by the Islamist group of El Nahdha, supported by USA, Qatar, and Saudi Arabia.

In late October, after ten months from Ben Ali's fall, the Islamist party Ennahda won the elections with a striking 40% consent. Then, Mohammed Sgaier Awlad Ahmed, one of the Tunisian best-known poets and contemporary writers, claimed that the Arab Spring was "A stolen revolution!" because

> "Here as much as in other places, Islamists have taken over power without deserving it. They have not played the slightest part in the riot! They only came out after January 14. They bought the votes of the lowest social classes with the money from Qatar, Saudi Arabia, and the US. Hungry citizens sold their vote for 30 dollars."

Once again, the "proxy war" strategy (the USA) returned on the stage. Saudi Arabia and Qatar put their plans in action through the Islamist party Ennhadha (Nhada) for the return of the original culture – the Islamic Wahhabism! During summer 2011, through the funds received by Saudi Arabia and Qatar, Nahdha sponsored the vast majority of weddings celebrated by Tunisian couples according to Islamic traditions. Furthermore, needy families received assistance through new social centers, so they could eat meals and pray in the same place. The pilgrimages to the Mecca (the Hajj - the fifth pillar of Islam, mandatory upon every Muslim) were doubled and offered free of charge. Within a year, the number of mosques increased from 2500 to 4000, and many of them celebrated their rituals according to the "Salafi" tradition, the most radical religious faith!

As a matter of fact, the US and Saudi Arabia worked hard to Islamize Tunisia after the Revolution. However, they failed in their purpose because Salafism twisted the mind of more than eight thousand young jihadists who went to fight in Syria (they are now members of ISIS) and more than three thousand in Libya joined Daëch. More young individuals continue to join terrorist groups, although the local governments are trying to contrast the phenomenon. In spite the efforts, in March 2015, some Tunisian

Jihadists attacked the Bardo Museum in Tunis killing 22 tourists (four Italians), and another fundamentalist murdered 37 people on the beach of Sousse (the victims were predominantly British and Belgians); once again, both terrorist groups were associated with Daëch Libya! Then, the State of Emergency declared by the Tunisian government led to the immediate closure of more than a hundred mosques that celebrated Salafi rites. Eventually, the police enacted the arrests of nearly 300 ultra-Orthodox Salafi, including 150 high-level officials and managers of the Tunisian Police Forces (Police and National Guard).

In spite of the national State of Emergency, terrorists of Al Qaeda Maghreb still kill soldiers of the ordinary army (the number of victims decreases every day), and they lead operations from the mountainous areas on the border with Algeria; furthermore, crime are continuously committed by the Tunisian foreign fighters belonging to ISIL in Libya!

Although the "Islamic-Orthodox" religion is visibly spreading around Tunisia, the Western world can hardly see that more than 20% of the population has fairly accepted the Salafi traditions, in the last years. The issue lies within the fact that Wahhabism promotes the return of a pure and uncontaminated culture, greater dedication and submission to the Koran, and the fight against corruption and the materialistic leadership of Western cultures, all of which can be used as justifications to indoctrinate new religious followers who may become jihadists.

On the one hand, Tunisians are well educated, and they do not easily accept other people's impositions. In particular, university students and teachers unanimously believe that the Tunisian Constitution enshrines in itself some of the most important International Human Rights. On the other hand, Tunisian Salafists are still like a soaring splinter in the back because they work together with the Islamic orthodoxy and with

"The Grand Mufti, who are Islamic theologians working in universities, and imams who preach in the most important mosques,

monarchies, and governments. This is the same Islamic orthodoxy with which the Catholic Church tries to create a dialogue."

With this statement, university teachers sent a message to all potential interlocutors, especially institutions. The involvement of the Catholic Church nullifies the positive effects of the interreligious dialogues that were promoted until today, because the Church is convinced that mutual respect comes only with mutual knowledge. In this way, Islamic followers do not come to reason with the Western world, because the two religions tend to highlight their differences.

This flawed thought is as much false as the demarcation line between the Muslim orthodoxy and fundamentalism. An increasing group of intellectuals proved with evidence that Saudi Arabia and the Islamic orthodoxy played a key role in the activity of proselytism in Tunisia. To contrast this activity, the Tunisian activist Faïza Skandrani Zouaoui (who died last year) coordinated the "Groupe d'appui à la parité", and she became the President of "Egalité et Parite" to promote gender equality in her country.

Today, both organizations still carry out her work as they wish to see realized an Islam that is not against gender equality, particularly when families have to deal with their legacies. Mohamed Talbi, one of the most famous modernist Islamic scholars, explained that a man had the right to receive "at least" twice more money than the woman from the family as part of his legacy (but, there is not a maximum limit!), while the Christian Bible was not granting anything to the woman. This topic could be better analyzed in another volume to discuss about inter-religious dialogue, but the Christian world safely ignores it because the Church does not want to raise a raucous.

The development of the modernist thinking has occurred after the Revolution, mainly affecting the Tunisian society; and, the rise of a critical sentiment characterized the new civil societies, which never fully developed their "critical thinking". In spite of this lost occasion, most of the Tunisian civil society worked extremely hard to achieve some successes, and Tunisia won Nobel Prize for Peace in 2015.

On August 14, 2012, all human rights organizations went down in the streets of Tunis together with ten thousand protesters including men, women, and children who, at the unison, established a strong opposition against the Islamists belonging to El Nahdha that were pressing the Tunisian Parliamentary Commission to include Art.28 in the new Constitution. This article would describe women as "supplementary" members of their families, but women built a strong opposition against this definition and they shouted that "[it is] A term that we do not understand", "There is no Republic without gender equality", and "Tunisian Women are complete women, plus another half."

The protest of the Tunisian civil society provided the opportunity to open a political "dialogue" with the most radical institutions (religious conservatism of Al Nahdha) through the foundation of special committees formed by university professors, intellectuals and representatives of associations. "The Quartet", the official name of the new committee won the Nobel Prize.

Certainly, the path to change Art.28 was neither easy nor short. On January 14, 2013, the new Constitution included gender equality rules. The two organizations called "Dialogue" and "Civil Society" obtained this great achievement through their hard work.

The media never broadcasted news about the negotiations among the parties, which occurred in the background during protests. Furthermore, the Constitution included a series of "gender-sensitive" articles promoted by the "Quartet" in a common framework of values and rules recognized by both the Islamists of Nahdha and the Tunisian Civil Society!

Today, Tunisia is following the path towards modernization that was defined already by Bourguiba in the sixties and seventies. Indeed, under Bourguiba, Tunisia experienced a period of modernization that stunned the Western countries; for example, he encouraged all the activities that could improve the life of women in the civil society.

In this context, the international community watched the rise of a specific Tunisian modernism. While Islamic modernism attempted to open a religious dialogue with the Western cultures, Bourguiba was trying to modernize the Islamic world from the inside out. The new candidate to the Presidency Essebsi and the leaving President Marzouki ran the elections in December 2014, and the event confirmed the dichotomies between Traditionalists (Orthodox) and modernists. Therefore, the history of Tunisia can unveil the background activities of this particular period.

In 1956, at the end of the colonial era, Tunisia gained its independence through a popular uprising led by Habib Bourguiba. Then, in 1956-1958, two religious and social trends began to dominate the Tunisian political scene, particularly the Orthodox Islam with Arab cultural origins, and the Mediterranean Modernism.

Therefore, "Bourghibism" still has a positive effect over Tunisia and the new "Civil Society" successfully introduced the concept of "modernity" in the country thanks to the application of social pressure.

The new innovative Constitution complies with the rules established by the UN Declaration of Human Rights (1948), in spite of the political pressures applied by the Islamist group of El Nahdha. In particular, the document says, "Tunisia is a civil State based on citizenship, the popular will, and the rule of law" and it includes "freedom of conscience", which cannot be fully realized because it is a principle running against the will of Islamic religion. Although Art. 46 of the Constitution recognizes the principle of equality between genders and the so-called civil society has become a part of the global civilization who accepted the culture of human rights and democracy, both Muslim men and women must respect the basic principles of the Arab-Muslim community, as El Nahdha demanded during the negotiations.

Western countries may have missed the following important information, or they may have interpreted it in the wrong way. *Tunisia is the only country in the Mediterranean area that has managed to find an institutional compromise between Islamic religious traditions and the modernist culture of civil society.*

The new generation of Tunisian intellectuals shows such a great interest in modernity that the international community may begin to talk about a new humanism for the Islamic world. Their education took place in the traditional context of local universities, but also in some of the most prestigious Western colleges in France, Italy, and Germany, where they learnt to combine harmoniously their "civil" duties together with their religious traditions.

President Obama and his State Department have never examined all these matters, and many other wonders of the historical heritage coming from the peoples of Islam have not been discovered, yet. The European Union has failed to learn more about Islam, too (*).

Although Tunisia has a modern and democratic Constitution, the country did not fully recovered from the Islamic wave that blew up the country for almost 3 years. Indeed, especially considering that thousands of Tunisians have chosen to side with ISIS, the worst days for the country may still have to come.

The Arab spring occurred in other countries, and the Tunisian experience seemed to repeat itself in Egypt. However, while Tunisian "modernism" pushed society to create better living conditions, the army and the General Abd al-Made al-Sisi took down (using military force) the Egyptian Islamic leader Morsi and the Muslim Brotherhood. In June 2014, the new Egyptian President Al Sisi delivered a speech to the highest authorities of the Islamic Sunni university/mosque of al-Azhar, and he proclaimed a religious reform, so he said

"The Muslim world can no longer be perceived as a source of anxiety, danger, death, and destruction for the rest of humanity. The Islamic religious leaders must 'get out of themselves' and favor a 'religious revolution' to eradicate bigotry, and they must replace it with a more enlightened 'view of the world'. If they do not do this, they will take their responsibility before God for having brought the Islamic community on the verge of ruin."

The Western and Christian worlds must learn this once-in-a-life lesson!

Note of the author (*): While I thought about Europe, my mind came up with the figurative meaning of "coglione" (from the Latin coleonem). This term may be read as "cum leo" (the lion). In detail, the person who fights a lion cannot help but watch the beast without understanding anything of what is actually happening around himself. Here and later, we will observe how Europe as a whole just did not understand what was happening during the Arab Spring.

Chapter VII – Comparing Libya and Syria: Gheddafi's Murder

After Tunisia and Egypt, "popular uprisings" also overwhelmed Libya. On February 15, 2011, the police arrested the human rights lawyer Fathi Terbil in Benghazi, who also legally represented the families of a thousand prisoners that the security forces of the Gaddafi regime massacred in 1996. The web became the social platform on which bloggers and opponents of the dictatorship began to gather.

On February 17, the Libyan young generations organized a demonstration in Benghazi and they called it *the day of wrath*; there, more than two thousand young people marched on the streets to demand "Justice and Freedom", and to protest against the arrest of Mr. Terbil. However, the security forces brutally fired on the crowd; and, the Libyan young generations hoped to exploit the horrible event to modernize their society through a revolt. Gaddafi did not give up, because he thought that he could crush the protest as it had already done many times. By the end of February, the regime killed 1500 individuals and it imprisoned 5000 protesters; therefore, Western democracies decided to organize a new intervention.

The United States, great eminence of the revolutionary logic in the Mediterranean, raised world public opinion against the heinous attacks of Gaddafi, whose air force mercilessly bombed the rebels and many civilians in Benghazi and in all major cities of Cyrenaica. The International Criminal Court (ICC), at the request of the USA (who have always refused to recognize this legal entity!), opened an investigation on the Libyan events and the outcomes of it were quickly brought to the attention of the UN Security Council. With the unconditional support of the Arab League, the United Nations approved resolution 1973 establishing a no-fly zone over Libya to protect civilians.

Then, the NATO intervention began on March 19. France attacked the defensive lines of Gaddafi from the sea. In few days,

Americans, British, and Italians destroyed the headquarters of Gaddafi in Tripoli as well as all command posts and Libyans communications; so, loyalists to the regime admitted their defeat.

The situation seemed to become more stable; then, by its own volition, France officially recognized the National Transitional Council (NTC) as the legitimate representative of Libya (rebels) and it proclaimed itself as the head of the Western coalition including Britain and Italy; the United States was puzzled about the actions carried out by France. The No Flay Zone imposed by the resolution did not work as initially intended, and the NATO coalition increased the size of its mission and it enlarged its own mandate. At the same time, Americans did not want to commit further military resource in the Middle East, because it wished to avoid other horrible experiences like Iraq and Afghanistan.

Once again, President Obama adopted the "proxy war" strategy. The White House demanded a military intervention to Saudi Arabia in Libyan territories, but the Saud rulers were also facing local Shiite uprisings. In fact, 20% of the Saudi population was Shiite and it took advantage of the winds of news from the Mediterranean to seek the renewal of the religious system according to the Sharia Law. However, Americans demanded financial support and the supply of small weapons to Libyan rebels, plus the permission of the "Arab League". With Bahrain on fire (the Shiites were in clear majority, and they no longer could tolerate the regime of the Sunni monarchy) and Iran under pressure, Riad accepted the procurement of armaments signed with the US. Therefore, military insurgents received weapons and other supplies through an agreement with Qatar, which took all the responsibility for the cargo.

Chapter VIII - Wahhabism in Saudi Arabia and Qatar

In order to understand some of the peculiarities of the Arab Spring, a comparative analysis of Saudi Arabia and Qatar becomes necessary. These two countries are the driving forces of the Gulf Cooperation Council (GCC), and they both attempt to contrast the Iranian political influence over their territories. Among the differences between them, there is the fact that Saudi Arabia is one of the largest countries in the world with 30 million inhabitants, while Qatar is as big as the Italian region called Marche, and it has a population of 2 million people (only three hundred thousand citizens have Qatari nationality). Additionally, Saudi Arabia and Qatar are in contrast due to the Iranian Shiite schism, which is the main reason of the profound and ancient rivalry between Sunnis and Shiites that continued to broaden over the decades until it reach its peak during the war in Yemen.

Diplomacy and international commitments between Saudi Arabia and Qatar, especially since 9/11, have always developed within these two realities (Sunni and Shiite); therefore diplomatic relations have always worked in a fast paced and ever-changing environment called the "Arab world", which often prefers to be identified as the "Arab League". Since the beginning of the last century, Saudi Arabia has been the world leader in the extraction and production of oil, while Qatar has become a leader in the field of natural resources only form the late nineties through to the discovery of large gas fields. Then, Qatar structurally organized its ambitious international politics with the profits obtained through the sale of gas.

In a matter of few years, Qatar has become one of the nations with most overseas investments, and it made itself well known as a regional mediator to the rest of the world through the media satellite channel *Al-Jazeera*. This channel often broadcasted news about the most dramatic phases of the jihadist war and terrorist attacks in the Middle East from the point of view of orthodox religious individuals or jihadists. In practice, Qatar developed social and economic relationships with Salafi leaders and active fundamentalists in the region, while continuing to present itself as a valuable economic partner for the United States and European countries. In detail, it settled preferential relations with the *Muslim Brotherhood* in Egypt, as well as with all the post-Islamic-revolution Salafi groups. In some cases, Qatar became the shelter of the Syrian opposition, al-Qaeda Iraq and Maghreb, although the United Nations had already included the name of these groups on a black list of terrorist groups.

Looking at what happened in the Arab world in the last decade, Riyadh and Doha applied diverse policies in accordance with the differences identified for each regional context - from Syria to Egypt, from Libya to Lebanon – and they adapted their own political strategies to respond to each situation. On the one hand, Saudi Arabia evidently supported President Mubarak and the current President Abd al-Made al-Sisi in Egypt; at the same time, Qatar provided financial and ideological support to the Muslim Brotherhood. On the other hand, since the beginning of the civil war, both nations are supporting rebel militias who fight against the regime of Bashar al-Assad in Syria.

Therefore, in some cases, Saudi Arabia and Qatar have different strategic approaches to expand their political influence in the region; in other cases, they develop a form of collaboration designed to support the strategic long-term common interests. Now, it is time to add the differentiating element that characterizes the interpersonal relationships among the members of the Arab League, in which Saudi Arabia has always acted as a catalyst for the Sunni orthodoxy (to which Qatar belongs, too). First, this paper analyses the relations between the King Abdullah bin Abdulaziz al Saud (his successor Salman bin Abdelaziz) and Gaddafi; then, it examines the case of the Alawite Assad.

In the first case, the international community assisted to the so-called *Arab hatred for Gaddafi*, which began in the assembly of the Arab League that immediately sided against the king of Jordan and Saudi Arabia, and in favor of Yasser Arafat for the sad Palestinian "black September". Gaddafi used to admire the ruler

Nasser of Egypt, who showed his the difference of character, style, and vision that would oppose him against the Orthodox Arab leadership, particularly the Gulf monarchies. Over time, Gaddafi obtained the titles of "King of the African Kings" and "the Dean of Arab leaders", due to his sarcastic and calculated provocations to the Arab world. Then, the blade on the green Saudi flag must have shimmered with emotion, because the time to implement the "law of retaliation" arrived when the Saud family was asked to lead a direct intervention against Gaddafi. This law is an essential element of the Saudi Arabian culture!

In the case of Syria, the situation was very different. Both Saudi Arabia and Qatar provided financial and logistical support to the Sunni armed opposition, and they performed a religious diktat towards Iran, which silently funded the Alawi regime of Assad (the Shiite Iran is the natural rival of the Sunni Wahhabism in Saudi Arabia and Qatar). The hatred between Arab Sunni and Iranian Shiite became evident in other international military scenarios.

In August 2010, the national equilibrium of Lebanon gave rise to a government of national unity under the leadership of the Premier Saadi Hariri. This "internal balance" was achieved through the strong diplomatic activity of Saudi Arabia and thanks to the imposed Syrian protection. In 2005, not identified killers assassinated the ex-President of Lebanon, Rafic Hariri (Saadi's father); in those days, the International Criminal Court (ICC) opened an investigation and formalized an act of official aggression.

Rumors were that the ICC intended to condemn a group of Hezbollah for the assassination. However, both the Saudi King Abdullah Abdelaziz and the Syrian President Bashar al Assad flew to Beirut to reach an agreement on the accusations moved against the right murderers. Saudi Arabia wished to charge the hypothetical responsible(s) for the murder of Hariri, but the Premier Assad marked the event as a destabilizing act that could cause the destabilization of the local government.

The two meeting leaders did not find a common agreement, and the press commented the event with a cold "no avail". Prime

Minister Hariri claimed, "The two leaders have arrived to Beirut on the same plane, but they went away taking different paths." Going into detail, President Assad talked with Abdullah for less than 5 minutes to explain him that Iran was behind the Hezbollah and Syria. Furthermore, Iran was ready to denounce the suspicious activities that Saudi Arabia carried out after the assassination of Hariri, because other four political figures (2 Hezbollah, a Christian Maronite and one Shiite) died in mysterious circumstances and the authorities did not solve the case, yet. The two leaders did not shake their hands and the ICC did not formalize the charges against the Hezbollah.

On that day, the Saudi Prince Abdullah gave Assad a sentence to death (the so-called fatwa!). Orthodox Islam does not forget anything; it gets its "fatwa" (revenge) soon or later; and, is it characterized by destructive alchemies of religious origins that are deeply rooted in its DNA.

Chapter IX – The Death of the American Ambassador Chris Stevens

At the beginning of July 2011, Qatar directly communicated to the US Department of State (Hillary Clinton) that it would send aid to the Sunni "Islamists" of Benghazi (which later turned out to be aggregated to Al Qaeda!), once it received the approval to support the rebels in Libya. The outcome of the war was uncertain and armed opponents were constantly taking control of the area. On August 19, the revolution arrived at the gates of Tripoli, after freeing many Libyan cities and having hoisted the tricolor flag - red, black, and green. Sirte was the last loyalist stronghold to fall, the last hiding place of the dictator. On October 20, Gaddafi was captured and brutally killed by the rebels; after three days, the CNT proclaimed the liberation of Libya, which suffered an eight-month-long war (according to CNT) and the death of thirty thousand victims, corresponding to slightly less than a fifth of the victims who died in Syria.

The comparison between the wars in Libya and Syria is more than legitimate, because there is ample evidence showing that the US have somehow participated to both conflicts. As soon as Gaddafi died, armed groups took possession of the country, and they re-introduced tribal traditions. The basic Committees of Gaddafi's Green Book returned into the hands of "Top Families" at the local level, so the situation was reaching its boiling point. The Libyan Premier, Abdullah Al Thani, claimed that the military situation was out of control, because members of Al Qaeda and Boko Haram joined the main terrorist groups operating in Libya. The naïve Western world thought that the fighting parties could reconcile and diplomatically achieve an agreement, but the long-awaited social and tribal negotiations never occurred.

The toughest international jihadism emerged from Syria and Iraq under the auspices of Qatar and Turkey (read - USA and Saudi Arabia), and several new outbreaks appeared in the area. The revolution completely deviated from its natural course and objectives, and the Special Commissioner of the United Nations stimulated the "militarization" of society and institutions, especially local ones. Officially, there used to be three armies in the country; first, the "regular" army, (ex-members of Gaddafi's personal guards), who copiously moved in Nigeria to found the group known as "Boko Haram Nigeria"; second, the army led by general "At Haftar" (who became the military coordinator of the 'legitimate' government in Tobruk); third, the Islamist army of "Fajr Libya." The latter is particularly important because it used to receive direct aid from Qatar.

Within a few months, from an initial base of Benghazi, Fajr Libya moved fast on the battlefields, so it occupied Tripoli and its surroundings. In his initial contacts with Qatar, the US Ambassador Stevens claimed that the Islamist group was his preferred. Once in Tripoli, Fajr Libya became the "Libyan Dawn Coalition", which officially supported the Egyptian Muslim Brotherhood (Qatar provides funds for both of them!), and Ansar Echariaâ Benghazi. Then, the new coalition aided the Libyan Islamist party that, in 2014, changed its name into the "New General National Congress".

Additionally, there used to be seven "minor" military groups operating in the areas of Cyrene and Tripoli. Ansar Echariaâ and Al Qaeda Maghreb owned four of these Islamist groups, which became part of "Daëch". In practice, the situation between Libya and Somalia was similar, but the US did not intervene in the former case. In fact, the US and NATO just launched a few missiles from a ship at the beginning of the conflicts.

On September 11, 2012, Ambassador Christopher Stevens and three members of his staff were massacred in Benghazi by a group of jihadists belonging to Ansar Echariaâ (reclaiming the act in 2014) while they were moving toward a CIA compound near the US Consulate that was repeatedly attacked by the revolutionists in Benghazi.

Nobody claimed the attack immediately, and the lack of a culprit highlighted the unusual behavior of the USA in this event. Why was Ambassador Stevens in Benghazi, if he was in office in

Tripoli? Why did he not receive adequate protection? Why militias had targeted the US Consulate in Benghazi? Why security guards had completely abandoned the area at the time of the attack? Why Ambassador Stevens was traveling to Benghazi, where the CIA had its agents? Too many questions that the White House itself has not been able to answer, if not raising another cloud of dust with the news that the "movements" of Benghazi were a popular reaction to the movie on Muhammad, which was directed in the US with American actors. Now, the film is under investigation for alleged slander against Islam.

The erroneous involvement of the US in the conflicts and its wrongdoings had a boomerang effect on the State Department and the CIA, and many events did not produced the desired outcomes. In October, Hillary Clinton resigned as Secretary of State and justified her "withdrawal" due to a bad hit on the head. Then, she disappeared from the American political scene from March 2013 until the re-election of Obama for a second term, and she promoted herself as the new leader of the Democrats for the elections in 2016.

Clinton's letter of resignation was rapidly followed by the one from the CIA Director, General David Petraeus (former commander of the forces for the liberation of Iraq and Afghanistan). He claimed that he made "a very serious mistake by engaging in a love affair out of his marriage. Such behavior is unacceptable, both as a husband and as the head of an organization such as the CIA." However, the events unveiled by the General were as old as the war in Iraq; and, all of a sudden, Petraeus felt compelled to confess details about his love affairs. Yet, no one ever thought that there could be interconnections between these two strange "resignations" and the events that occurred in Benghazi!

On May 24, 2013, an American "diplomatic source" showed evidence to the international newspapers of the *Wall Street Journal*, *Washington Post* and *The Daily Beast* of the mysterious events that took place in Benghazi. According to the same source, Stevens was leading a secret mission on behalf of the CIA that had very little to do with diplomatic relations, because it was about American "realpolitik". News revealed that the CIA in Benghazi "had the task of preventing the risk of terrorist attacks" by curbing extremist infiltrations in a country that was already in a state of chaos after the death of Gaddafi, and controlling the allocation of the weapons founded by rebels in state deposits.

The Secretary of State herself, Hilary Clinton, probably commissioned this secret mission; she ordered the recovery of these weapons to Petraeus and she demanded to move them in Syria, where the opposition forces to Assad had already reported the lack of supplies from Qatar. However, these weapons had to pass through Turkey; in this case, Ambassador Stevens found an agreement with Abdelkarim Belhadj, who was his main contact with Libyan rebels during the war in 2011. Therefore, when Stevens arrived in Benghazi, the CIA attempted to disarm the Libyan rebels, who violently reacted with a real revolt that reached its peak in the assault to the consulate. The rebels craved full political autonomy as they intended to influence the domestic policies of Islam, and they wished to serve as "guardians of the Islamic revolution" in Libya.

The Libyan war and its course are reported in the introductory article. Although the media and other strong political powers dropped a curtain of silence on this international conflict, Europe (in particular) knew that the situation was dramatic. In this general chaos, the parliamentary government of Tobruk, supported by General Khalifa Haftar, successfully emerged as the most secular and legitimate authority over the country. The second authority in the country was led by a radical formation that was based in Tripoli; yet, this formation was vaguely similar to the Islamist opposition whose members used to come from the organization Ansar al Sharia, which is still supported by Qatar today.

Bernardino Leon, the Commissioner of the United Nations in Libya, has been working for a whole year as a mediator to reach an agreement between the two opposing factions for the reconstruction of the country. However, the decisions of multiple local actors cannot be linked to those of the two main coalitions. Tribal culture gave rise to autonomous militias in many cities of the Fezzan that are influenced by Al Qaeda Maghreb; similar militias were organized from the southern areas of Cyrenaica and Tripolitania to the borders with Chad and Niger, where Boko Haram and other groups are still operating.

In early October, Bernardino Leon announced the formation of a "National Agreement Government" to reorganize peacefully Libya. Nevertheless, social tension is still high because the National Council of Elders, which represents the real tribal subdivision of Libyan society, is not involved in the peace process. In addition, the international community have to fear the shadow of terror that the Islamic States (Daëch) can expand due to its ability to recruit new members within other radical groups. ISIS is still active in Libya because there are groups who chose to swear allegiance to the Caliphate in exchange for the global legitimacy of a local jihad. Thus, these groups modify the meaning of "jihadism" to shout their general discontent and dissatisfaction with the internal situation, rather than promoting real theological extremism. This new jihadism is a sort of "functional jihadism" rather than doctrinal.

Beyond any possible future scenario, Libya repeated the stiff diplomatic and geopolitical mistakes that were made by the Obama administration. From the single-core strategies implemented by Bush Jr. (Afghanistan and Iraq), the US is usually forced to apply the "proxy war" model that was adopted during the Soviet-Afghan war. Then, in 2013, the National Intelligence Council officially confirmed that Obama's preferred strategy was the "Stay Behind" model. In *Global Trends 2030*, Keith Alexander - head of the National Security Agency (NSA) - writes in the preface that the United States will have to learn to be "first among equals" in the early future. In fact, the events occurred in the Mediterranean area shows that "the unipolar moment is over and the 'Pax Americana', the era of US dominance in international politics that began in 1945, has definitely run out."

In May 2014, the institutionalization of the "proxy war" model followed Obama's speech at West Point, where he pointed out that "America must lead the world stage. At the same time, the United States' military action cannot be the only or even the first component of our leadership, every time and in each case. Just because we have the best hammer does not mean that every nail should be a problem." In practice, the US is not anymore the police officer of the world, but it becomes "the major actor" of the "Stay Behind" strategy.

Chapter X - The Syrian Improvisation

The case of Syria was introduced earlier in this book, when I wrote about the Libyan armaments that had to be carried towards Aleppo. This intervention confirmed the "Stay Behind" strategy of the White House, which improvised a military intervention to defend its interests in the area. The United States could not rely neither on Saudi Arabia nor on Qatar, in contrast to what happened in other Mediterranean countries affected by the Arab revolutions. In fact, the last meeting held by the Arab League had highlighted the incompatibility between the Alawi pro-Assad Syria and the guidelines issued by the Saudi Sunni. Furthermore, as a result of the "confrontation" between Assad and the of King Arabia about the danger avoided by the Hezbollah for the ICC investigation on the murder of the Lebanese Prime Minister Hariri, an under-cover American intervention might look like a clear declaration of war against Iran, which has always been an ally of Syria.

In addition, the Syrian authorities firmly resisted against the rise of a popular rebellion, which took place in the northern Sunni Syria thanks to the considerable support and legitimacy given by the Syrian population. Just this fact became an obstacle to the implementation of the "proxy war" model adopted in Libya (pseudo-revolutionaries aided by Western air strikes). The situation was completely different in Syria, where large segments of a multi-religious society (Alawites, Sunnis, Shiites, and Christians) used to be held precariously together by the charisma and the secular cultural background of President Assad. Syria has its own civil identity that differentiates it from all other nations in the Mediterranean area. Therefore, the Americans preferred to help in the processes of recruiting, training, equipping, and deploying Islamic mercenaries in Syria by passing through Turkey, which became the regional area for soldiers' transit.

Hence the US, taking advantage of the fact that the Sunni opposition against Assad found hospitality in Qatar (like all the Sunni jihadist groups!), held the first meeting to support the Syrian Revolution in Doha, and it invited the European Union at the table of "aids". In October 2011, the EU and the foreign representative Mrs. Ashton expressed their concerns and no national representatives attended the first meeting, given the different political views that existed about Syria. The meeting sponsored by the Arab League gave immediate results, so that loans were authorized for the Syrian National Council (SNC - located in Turkey) and for the creation of the Free Syrian Army (FSA - the right hand of the SNC). In December 2011, hundreds "Libyan and Tunisian Salafi" volunteers, who are currently operating in Homs, Idlib, and Rastan, formed the jihadist core belonging to FSA (they are now better known as ISIS foreign fighters!). In 2012, the FSA – funded by Qatar, Saudi Arabia, and the US – had more than 15,000 militiamen of Saudi, Libyan, Tunisian (4000 Tunisians!) and Egyptian origins, aiming to bring together all extremist groups under the aegis of the SNC. However, many militiamen joined the ranks of ISIS as soon as the Caliphate stepped into the Syrian territories. Successively, in 2012, one year after the first meeting in Doha, I wrote the following article about Syria.

(The Opinion, November 14, 2012 - A window on the future of Syria in Doha). Syria is the keystone of a US / Saudi Arabia Cold War against Iran. ... Syria is the hub of the most dangerous issues in the Middle East, including the security of Lebanon and Israel, and the persisting religious confrontation between Iran and Saudi Arabia. In Syria, the Sunni opposition has silenced the different pacifist social parties, because the latter initially emerged as a union of democrats in contrast with the regime of Bashir Al Assad; furthermore, the Free Syrian Army (FSA) and the regular Syrian Army have increased their inhuman actions and violent military operations. Since December 2011, hundreds of Salafi Tunisian volunteers independently acted from the FSA, because they joined Homs, Idlib and Rastan. President Sabra, who is a catholic and the leader of SNC, has the duty and mission of bringing these extremist groups under the aegis of the SNC.

Today, Syria is the key element to maintain the alliance between the US and Saudi Arabia, which was triggered by the famous speech of President Obama in Cairo, in June 2009. Furthermore, Syria is now the common matrix of the various "revolutions" bursting in the Arab Mediterranean countries. On that occasion, Obama spoke of new regional powers (Saudi Arabia and Qatar) and the joint struggle against Islamic terrorism and Iran.

Saudi Arabia and Qatar are the real military moneylenders of the Free Syrian Army and foreign Salafi groups that support the FSA. Ultra-Orthodox Sunni think that Syria is just a pawn of their campaign against the Shiite Iran secessionists of the Ayatollahs.

As opposed to the axis USA / Saudi Arabia, Syria and Al Assad have relied on Russia and Iran. The skirmishes over the Strait of Hormuz and the Persian Gulf are just a microscopic part of a dangerous cold war between Tehran and Riyadh; the "energy-based" alliance between Iran and Russia confirms this assumption. The oil coming from the Caspian countries is transported to refineries in northern Iran, and then it is exported through the Persian Gulf and the Mediterranean, through the terminal in Syria. In essence, everything suggests that behind the US political openness towards Islam, there is a war against Iran on the "energy control" in that area.

However, on the Syrian home front, the anti-Assad opposition is crumbling down, despite the apparent unity, due to increasing differences among its members, while the Salafi are warning that Assad will live the same fate of Muammar Gaddafi.

The two opposing parties crave to win the civil war while the humanitarian emergency is broadening. Thirty-five thousand victims - mostly civilians - died in this conflict; yesterday, more than ten thousand Syrian refugees have crossed the border with Turkey. The United Nations estimates that over four million Syrians will need aid by 2013; many of these refugees already live in the camps located in Jordan, Lebanon, and Turkey.

The post-election President Obama.../...after the scandals of the State Department and the CIA, suggested a more cautious intervention in favor of the Syrian opposition forces. In particular, the international community could probably start talking about a "ceasefire" and the beginning of diplomatic relations among the different factions, if the US cuts the delivery of armaments, and Saudi Arabia stops the flow of funds to the Salafis. Otherwise, the fratricidal Syrian conflict is doomed to become a "Civil War" that will bring more death and destruction. In the next few days, political-strategists will understand whether the Syrian crisis is set to expand in the Persian Gulf.

As it is well known, the US drastically reduced the support for war materials to the forces of FSA, but Saudi Arabia did not veto the flow of funds. Furthermore, the situation became more dangerous when ISIS joined into the already existing conflict. On June 29, 2014, the Islamic State proclaimed the birth of the "Caliphate" and it became fully autonomous because it seceded from the control of Al Qaeda; the attention of the international institutions moved back on Iraq, which had become more Shiite and less multi-ethnic.

Since the Islamic State (ISIS) stepped into Syrian territory, only few people noticed that Iraq and Iran were re-gaining a considerable strategic role on the international stage. The Kurds earned an undeniable autonomy in the northern part of the country, while the Sunni minority that created Al Qaeda in Iraq was almost marginalized and severely under-represented in the Iraqi parliament. Sunni terrorism intensified its operations for this reason, and it built the foundations for the realization of the Islamic State. Clearly, the Shiite-led Baghdad became almost dependent from Tehran, and the presence of irregular Shiite militias who fought against ISIS had further isolated Sunni tribes in the area.

The power of attraction exercised by Tehran, given the success achieved in Iraq, had involved Syria too, which used to receive the support from Hezbollah and Russia (common ally). In August, Russia, Iran, Iraq, and Syria created a joint military center to coordinate all the operations against ISIS in Iraq and Syria. From Baghdad, high officials thought about a large-scale Russian direct military intervention to contrast the caliphate in Iraq.

Furthermore, when Tehran signed the agreements on nuclear production, the local government claimed

> "As long as the United States will continue to support our rivals in the Middle East, like Saudi Arabia, our policy will continue to be of full support to our traditional allies, particularly with Syria because of the energy agreements already in place. Until yesterday, Iran has been always on the defensive in Syria, in Iraq, in the Gulf, and in Afghanistan, thanks to the strong presence of Sunnis in the area. Now, thanks to oil and gas revenues that will certainly grow because the UN has stopped the embargo through a nuclear deal, the country can exercise more freely its influence in the region. Therefore, Iran will restrain the "neo-Ottoman" expansionism of

Erdogan in Syria, Iraq, in the Caucasus, and central Asia; moreover, Iran will strongly oppose against the Saudis' Salafi-Wahhabi pan-Arabism in North Africa, in the Gulf, in Syria, and Iraq through the Sunni jihadists operating in those countries and areas" - Blitzquotidiano

The Kurdish issue is among the priorities of Iraq, too. The moderate Iraqi Kurds autonomously fight against their enemy, and they are increasingly closing to the Marxist Syrians (linked to the Kurdish PKK in Turkey). Therefore, the creation of a new independent Kurdish state may occur, in accordance with what will happen in Syria. Turkey, of course, does not like this hypothesis, but Russians and Iranians might seek to endorse the Kurdish independence movement to acquire a geo-strategic and powerful energy partner.

Eventually, the religious multiculturalism of the Kurdish populations is a key factor that should not be underestimated. In general, a pacifist background that is rooted in the Zoroastrian Kurdish diaspora of Yazidis unites the population, who does not belong to monotheism, and it has certainly influenced the expansion of Sunni and Shiite Islam. Just like Christianity and other monotheistic groups, this Kurdish diaspora has blended everything into a cultural crucible in which the religion, regardless of theological differences, promotes individuals' inner reflection, and social union. Even if President Obama (and his theory of generalized chaos) does not welcome the hypothesis of a united Kurdistan and he tries to contrast the idea, he would favor the complete annihilation of multi-confessional states, which used to characterize the entire Middle East before the war in Iraq.

Among the Republican candidates in the upcoming primary elections, Donald Trump is the most acclaimed representative of the party, because he would like to apply the "non-intervention" policy in the Middle East (perhaps rightly), and he claims that the West should "let the Syrians jump on the throats of each other". Although the presidential elections will happen next year and the current President may still order to the CIA to provide funds and training to "insurgents", I hope that Barack Obama has realized from his experiences in the Middle East that trying to combine reliable guerrilla groups have always ended miserably.

Now that the almost irrefutable theory of possible pacification in this infamous scenario belonging to the Middle East has been clarified, the international community must ask why Europe was the "great absent" in these revolutions and wars that mostly took place in the Mediterranean area. The reason can be found in the introductory article; Europe knows nothing about Islam and its religious traditions; therefore, Islam is "the Other", the foreigner, the unknown, and the feared one. Eventually, Europe does not have the slightest knowledge of the different Islamic conceptions of social status that are in place in most Muslim countries.

Chapter XI – The Orthodoxy of Islam and Islamic Fundamentalism

In the previous chapters, the most broad and general differences between the various forms of Islam have been highlighted, examined, and successfully remarked. In detail, Islam is divided in two main religious communities, the Sunni and the Shiite, which always fought against each other since the death of the Prophet Mohamed to decide who had to fill the role of Islamic spiritual and political leader. According to the Shiites, the new leader had to be a descendant of Muhammad's family, while, according to the Sunnis, one of the "friends of the Prophet" (Al Salafi Assaliho = hence the name Salafis) had to guide the community because they had lived side by side to Muhammad, and they had absorbed his knowledge and way of living. Indeed, Islam maintains its entirety in both the sacred texts of the Koran and the Sunna; and, it is only through the practice of Islam that one can understand the differences in the interpretations and practical applications of God's law (Sharia) in the two main beliefs. In detail, there are two distinct ways to practice religion in social life.

First, the Shiites have a well-organized "clergy" who regularly celebrates religious traditions. On the top of the hierarchical pyramid, there is the Imam, who is the leader of the Ayatollah (only for the first twelve!). Then, there are Religious Leaders working as political and spiritual guides for the entire community; they are scholars in theological and legal sciences, and they exert heavy influence over governmental policies and civil society. Each Ayatollah owns a private school where he educates the "mullah", who read and comment the Friday prayer.

The second difference is related to the legal and procedural aspects for the application of the Sharia. According to the Shiites, the only valid Legal school is the Jafarita, which is set on modernist criteria and it does not accept the *imitation* of dead lawyers. Therefore, lawyers who are still alive constantly update the law in relation to how they "interpret" the new theological cases. Moreover, the Shiite scholars of religious sciences give much more importance to *the practice of reason and intellect* than the Sunni; in fact, Sunnism forbids *it*, and it does not exist at all in the most perverse Wahhabism! The 'Ulema' (scientists and scholars of Islamic sciences) or muftis (Islamic academics whose ability to interpret the law is recognized by law, the Sharia) undertake the effort to interpret the sources of the law and deliver qualified legal opinions, giving rules to the religious followers and informing them on the legality of their actions.

On the contrary, there is not a real Clergy for the Sunni. The Sunni Arab world is teeming with Shuyukh (they are similar to the Ulema for the Shiite) who are not entitled to educate religious followers; therefore the Shuyukh is just a social honorific title. Still, sages and scholars (Ulema, muftis, mullahs) dominate the religious discourse with their sermons, in particular on the internet and television. Only some of them have attended faculties at the so-called Islamic Universities (Zituna in Tunis - Al Azhar in Cairo); in practice, Sunni scholars have to study by themselves.

Furthermore, there are four types of Law Schools (fiqh), including the Maliki, Shafiita, Hanbali, and Hanafi, which date back to the twelfth century. The ideas of Sunni Islam are as old as these schools! The *orthodox* Sunni Islam is the outcome of the reforms imposed by the Saudi Wahhabism in 1700; then, the Islamic reformism of the XIX century led to the formation of *Salafism*. In the elaboration of Islamic laws, the Sunni *forbids the practice of reason and intellect*, because they believe in the *taqlid* conceived as *acceptance, imitation, and emulation* of the Koran and Sunna.

The greatest flaw of the Islamic world is the impossibility to separate the state from religion! On the one hand, Turkey (thanks to Ataturk), Tunisia ("Quartet", Nobel Prize for Peace 2015), Iran, and Iraq have managed to separate these two powers. On the other hand, the rest of the Muslim world - including countries like Malaysia, Indonesia, India, and others - is naturally inclined to follow the Arabian orthodoxy, despite the fact that each country is free to adapt the Saudi Wahhabism to its own traditions and culture. In other words, each State is worthy of having its own autonomy and identity.

At last, there is the Islamic State (ISIS) promoting the foundation of the Caliphate. The major difference between the Sunni and ISIS is that the latter aims to restore the Islamic religion at its origins by uniting all the "conquered" territories under the Caliphate's banner. ISIS is an Islamist terrorist group that was founded in the northern side or Iraq; but it is better known for its operations in Syria and Iraq. Its current leader, Abu Bakr al-Baghdadi, has extended the Caliphate to all the territories fallen under his control (thus including the Libyan cities of Derna and Misurata). Through to conquest of the Libyan territories, the Arabic acronym has become "Daëch", which literally means "ad-Dawla al-Islamiyya al-fī'Iraq wa l-Sham", and it corresponds to the English expression "Islamic State of Iraq and al-Sham". Thus, the international community looks at the rise of "the Islamic State of Iraq and the Levant" (ISIL).

Chapter XII – Obama's Doctrine and the Islamic Fundamentalism in the Mediterranean Area and Middle East

On December 15, 2015, the American President Obama asked to the Sunni countries to promote more interventions against Islamic terrorism. Promptly, as the leading government of the Arab world, the Saudi Arabian Minister of Defense Mohamed bin Salman announced the coalition of at least 34 Sunni countries; and, all operations will be coordinated from the headquarter located in Riyadh. In his speech, the Minister pointed out that the coalition includes "a group of Islamic countries accounting for most of the Arab world" that are determined to fight against "the disease that affects the entire international community, not only the Arab Muslim world." Saudi Arabia and other five countries are already in a coalition to fight the "Holy War" against the Shiite Houthi rebels in Yemen. The new coalition will include Jordan, UAE, Pakistan, Bahrain, Bangladesh, Benin, Turkey, Chad, Togo, Tunisia, Djibouti, Senegal, Sudan, Sierra Leone, Gabon, Somalia, Guinea, the Palestinian national Authority, Comoros, Cote d'Ivoire, Kuwait, Lebanon, Egypt, Libya, Maldives, Morocco, Mauritania, Niger, Nigeria, and Yemen.

How and where this coalition will intervene is still unknown; furthermore, it may be hard to find other allies against Daëch, especially in Syria where Russian forces intervened on the side of the Shiite Assad and Lebanese Hezbollah. In fact, Vladimir Putin promptly reiterated, "in theory, the formation of a coalition brings positive effects, but the international community must see the outcomes of the interventions to make an evaluation." Putin and I have a similar point of view in this complicated matter. In particular, I have been preaching for some time that Al Zarqaui (the Caliph of Daëch!) spawned from the most fundamentalist Sunnism of Saudi Arabia; by comparison, Saudi Arabia favored the rise of Bin Laden and Al Qaeda in perfect agreement with the US and the CIA. Furthermore, after the fall of the regime led by Saddam, the CIA provided training and funds to Al Zarqaui to organize a group of Sunni jihadists who had to fight against the Kurdish in northern Iraq. Then, why the Saudis moved against the ISIL (Islamic State in Iraq and the Levant = Daëch)? The reasons can be found by looking at the following data.

Comparison List: Orthodoxy and Islamic Fundamentalism

System of Reference

- Saudi Arabia: Koran and Sunna – The Koran is the "Constitution" of the Country

- ISIL/Daech: Koran and Sunna

Judicial System

- Saudi Arabia: Sharia Law and the Jurists (fiqh)

- ISIL/Deach: Sharia Law. Self-managed by individual jihadists

Institutions and Authorities

- Saudi Arabia: The King is the Head of State and Government. He is also the Religious Leader, and the Prince of the Two Holy Mosques (Mecca and Medina)

- ISIL/Daech: The Caliph is the only authority

Legislative System

- Saudi Arabia: The King promotes laws together with the Royal Islamic Council (90 people elected by the King according to tribal traditions)

- ISIL/Daech: Self-management – based on the Sharia Law of the Caliph. Anarchic-theocratic system

Death penalty

- Saudi Arabia: "Decapitation", "shooting" or "stoning" in public (137 death penalties confirmed in 2015)

- ISIL/Daech: "Cutting the throat" of the victim, according to the opinion of the individual jihadist

Corporal Punishment

- Saudi Arabia: Law imposes them and they are carried out in public: cutting the hand (thieves), whipping, beatings, stoning and crucifixion

- ISIL/Daech: Every jihadist is both the Judge and Executor. Women can be enslaved!

"Freedom" and Human Rights

- Saudi Arabia: Islam is the only religion. There is no freedom. Islam is complete submission to the Law of God. Absolute prohibition to build religious buildings of other confessions. Political parties are not allowed!

- ISIL/Daech: There are no rights, except the duties imposed by the Sharia Law!

Inviolability of Islamic territory

- Saudi Arabia: No other religion is allowed; only Islam practices are permitted. 15% of the Saudi population is Shiite (helped and persecuted at the same time)

- ISIL/Daech: There is only the "Sunni Islam". Other territories are "war zones that need to be Islamized!"

Professed Confession

- Saudi Arabia: Orthodox and Conservative Sunnis coming from the Hanbali Law School (technical and moral

intransigence with a severe and ascetic lifestyle). Protectors of "the house" of Islam, which in this case is Saudi Arabia

- ISIL/Daech: "Salafist" Sunni movement (from *salaf* = *pious ancestors*). Purposes: **1)** to implement the Islamic Sharia in all communities; **2)** to unify the countries of Islamic faith in a single theocratic reality, under the guidance of the "Caliph"; **3)** the Islamization of the entire world to prepare the event of the Resurrection

On the one side, Saudi Arabians place themselves at the top of the Sunni Islamic world (in theory) because the Saudi King is also the responsible, as Prince of the two mosques, of the holy land for the whole Islam; thus, he is the main political and religious figure for the Umma (although the Shiite disagree on this aspect). On the other side, Daëch aims to unify all the Islamic countries in one single Islamic state governed by the Caliph, as it used to be with the Salafi Umayyad Caliphate (the first tribe that governed the Umma after the death of the Prophet Muhammad). It is clear as daylight that the Saudis fear the advance of Daëch, and they shake at the very idea that new Caliphate could subjugated them. It is for these reasons that the Saudis called to rally their "Arab" brothers. Finally, the comparison and contrast analysis has highlighted the substantial differences between the Orthodox Saudi Arabia and the "fundamentalist" politico-religious Daëch; the first aims to remain the religious leader of the Sunni world, while the second has its origins in the "Salafi" movement of the XIX century.

The doctrine professed by Al Baghdadi and the Caliphate is not very different from the Saudi Salafism, as shown in the chart. For example, in both doctrines, all Muslims followers must pledge allegiance to a single Muslim leader, just like Wahhabism used to demand an oath to the prophet Mohammed and his followers, even at the cost of their own life. According to ISIS' Wahhabi interpretation of the Sharia Law, that is much more radical than the one implemented in Saudi Arabia and in Qatar, "those individuals who do not obey to the law of God and do not give the oath of submission

80

must be killed, his wives and her daughters must be raped, and his goods must be confiscated."

The Sunni focus their attentions on the life of the Prophet, as it is *strictly* stated in both the Koran (in many verses God makes direct reference to the Prophet) and in thousands of Hadith. However, the substantial "difference" between the Sunni and the Shiite Islam springs from this interpretation of the Sharia Law. In particular, the Shiite fully recognize the Hadith of Mohammed and of his life, but they also acknowledge the judicial authority of the 12 Imam in the Islamic world. This important detail highlights another element to this topic; indeed, the Shiite interpretation of the Sharia Law does not stop to the life of the Prophet (as it is for the Sunni), because it is updated over time through the interpretations given by the various Imams. This detail is extremely important, because the Shiite cleric Nimr al-Nimr was decapitated in early January 2016 in Riyadh for *sedition and state terrorism*. His sermons were going against the conservative principles promoted by the *Shura Council*, which actually implements Islamic laws in Saudi Arabia.

By contrast, the most orthodox view of Salafism prohibits the interpretations of the sacred texts. *God's revelations and Mohammed given interpretations with his "examples" (the Sunni Hadith) are intangible, authentic, well founded, effective, and untouchable.* As the outcome of these observations, the main enemies of Sunni Islam are the Shiite, the Sufism (too transcendent!), all other Muslim schools that have consolidated practices like the visit to the tomb of the Prophet or to Marabut (burial place of the Holy Muslims), and the two other monotheistic religions. Although Sunni and Shiite have some similarities, but a different dogmatic nature, Fundamentalism is unlike them in the application of strategies. In fact, ISIL aims to subdue all Muslim societies under the Caliphate's banner, and it refuses doctrinal differences on the Salafist conception of the origins!

The Sunni religion and the Saud institutionalization of Wahhabism led to associate the idea of a "sovereign authority, two mosques" with the very same Saudi Kingdom (Medina and Mecca, the two locations where the Prophet died and was born, are still considered the pearls of the Islamic religion). ISIL has declared war against the Crown, perhaps reacting to this "bastardization" of the original Wahhabism, most probably because Saudi Arabia is an ally of the Western countries and it sells them local petroleum (Osama bin Laden declared war on the Saudis too, after the UN war in Afghanistan). Therefore, the differences between ISIS and Saudi Arabia are based on their conflicts of interest and lust for power throughout the Sunni world. Equally interesting, and much more diversified is the world of the Sunni Salafi Jihadism.

The Talibans are Afghan and Pakistani Koranic students who are usually associated with the Indian Deobandi School, which is a conservative Puritan movement inspired to the Saudi Salafism; in spite of their link, the Talibans keep their own identity and autonomy. The Deobandi School is the second most important institute in the world, right after the al-Azhar University in Cairo. In particular, the Deobandi School encourages the total adherence to the Sharia Law, and a strictly conservative interpretation of the Koran and the Sunna. In Pakistan, the Talibans sympathize for ISIL, differentiating themselves from their Afghan brothers who stay loyal to Al Qaeda and the Saudi Arabian approach.

Hence, there is a substantial difference between the *"dark side" of Saudi Arabia* known as *Al Qaeda* (The Royal Family never admitted that there are some Saudi families who provided funds and other resources to terrorists), and the Islamic State ISIL that inspires other groups of jihadists with its actions. On the one hand, ISIL has already become a source of inspiration for *Ansar Al Sharia* in Libya and Tunisia; *Al Qaeda in the Islamic Maghreb*, including Algeria, Libya, Tunisia, Mali, Nigeria; *Ansar Bayt Al Maqdis* in Egypt; *Boko Haram* in Nigeria; and, *the Talibans in* Pakistan. On the other hand, *Al Qaeda* identifies itself in the group of *Al Qaeda in the Arabian Peninsula* that is located in Yemen; this group controls *Al Shabaab* in Somalia, the *Afghan Talibans* and other groups scattered mostly in the African area of *Sahel, Algeria, Niger, Sudan, Ethiopia, Kenya* and other countries.

The dark side of Saudi Arabia also provides support, armaments, and funding to the Islamist opposition army in Syria and

Libya, directly or indirectly through Qatar. In addition, Saudi Arabia, supported by the US, rejects its responsibility at the UN for causing the mass migration of "Syrian refugees" who ask for asylum in the EU! At this point, the question is "who is holding the true divine message?" the jihadists who "sacrifice" their victims in the name of a powerful and merciful Allah, or the proselytism involving over a billion people who give priority to their own lives? Another problem also lies in the thousands of Islamic "variants"; Islam is a monotheistic religion, but it branches into different interpretations that multiply indefinitely in the absence of a real ecclesial framework, and religious followers normally have the ability to think critically about the readings of the Koran, except the Iranian Sunni.

Recently, the Western governments have accustomed the Western world to recognize the two main Islamic communities, Sunni and Shiite groups. Among the Sunnis, there are the self-proclaimed Caliphate of al Baghdadi, the Muslim Brotherhood in Egypt, the Libyan Islamists, Tunisians, Algerians, and Africans. On the contrary, the Shiites include the Alawites of Saddam and Assad, the Hezbollah, and the front of the Shiite Yemeni Houthi Zaydi. However, the real situation is more complicated than what it appears to be; and, experts have to collect more information and analyze it in order to unveil the mysteries of the Muslim world. When the Western cultures look at Islam, they believe that Islam has one purpose and one vision. However, if an individual enters into the galactic maze of Islam, he will be able to understand that the Islamic culture is quite complex. Ironically, the common factor among Islamic cultures is that they are all "different" from one another; indeed, each culture is unique and it wants to keep its individuality.

These differences include the theocratic and doctrinal approach; the diversity caused by the influence of Persian, Byzantine, and Greek cultures; the considerable dissimilarities in the legal systems (the Sunni have four legal systems); the social changes produced by the legacy of local traditions, or due to the period of "colonization". There are many other differences among the Islamic societies, who (deceitfully) emphasize, "ISIS, as well as the set of Salafi Jihadists, is not Islam!" However, only the West can recognize the authority of this statement. The "differences" that are highlighted in this chapter are solely applied within the Muslim world. Therefore, the same "differences" become a source of unity for the Islamic communities when Islam itself is questioned by the Western world.

After the 9/11 attacks, the Arab world and the peoples of the Islamic religion began to re-examine their identity. On June 12, 2009, an unexpected and unimaginable "awakening" called the "rebirth" (to Nahdha, in Arabic) of the Islamic-Arab sentiment followed Obama's speech to the brothers of Islam. All Muslim peoples, particularly those belonging to the Middle East, felt the need to create the conditions for the advent of a new Arab-Islamic "humanism"; then, this shared sentiment triggered the revolutions and promoted new changes in all Arab countries. However, the important developments in the whole area - including the advent of new Islamic democracies, and the burst of civil wars in Iraq, Syria, Libya, and Yemen – pointed out the gruesome elements of the duality, duplicity, and radicalization in the interpretation of Islam.

On the one hand, there are the Caliphate, Saudi Arabia, and Iran (which shows some differences); on the other hand, the Islamic modernism mainly promoted by Tunisia and Morocco ventured on a path of integration between peoples, after these two countries signed and ratified the UN Declaration on Human Rights. At the same time, some persistent and intolerable social conditions still afflict Tunisia, and the Western cultures cannot accept this situation. Moreover, the terrorist attacks at the Bardo Museum in Tunis and in Sousse, the presence of jihadists on the mountains at the border with Algeria, and the nearly eight thousand jihadists of Daëch in Syria and Libya, have fostered the return of radial Salafism.

After the last few episodes, the Tunisian Government has closed 80 Salafi mosques and it is aims to reintroduce the death penalty for crimes of terrorism, claiming that officers arrested and charged of acts of terrorism more than four hundred "recidivist" criminals in two months. Above all, the high percentage obtained by *Al Nhadha* (Islamist party) to the general election of 2012 was stunning; in fact, 40% of voters was favorable to the radicalization of the Islamic traditions in Tunisia. Certainly, this value alone does not mean that five million Tunisians are Salafis, or that there is a tiny minority of Jihadists among the Salafis.

Yet, the situation gets complicated with the analysis of the "propensity" of Islamic followers who become fundamentalists. In other words, the international community should wonder whether ISIL will arrive in Tunisia or not do it; furthermore, the proselytism in Qatar and Saudi Arabia has strengthened the concept of a theocratic State, which initially shifted from 10% (Bourguiba period) to 15% (during the dictatorship of Ben Ali); then this value skyrocketed to 40% in 2012. Will all Tunisians be happy to "go back to the origins" of Islam?

Well, the answer is already written in the history of the Mediterranean area, as well as that in all the peoples of Islamic origin. Actually, the radicalization of Islam periodically occurred in the Islamic world. For example, the Saudi El Wahab (1703-91), the Lebanese Rida (1865-1935), the Egyptian Hassan el Banna (1906-1966), the Egyptian Sayyid Qutb (1906-1966), the Iranian Shiite Ali Shariati (1933-1977), and the Ayatollah Khomeini (1902-1989), used to be scholars of the most extremist and fundamentalist Salafism. Delivering their ideologies, they inspired jihadist movements such as the *Muslim Brotherhood* in Egypt (1928 - Present!), *the Revolution in Persia* in the late 80's, the *Algerian FIS* in the 80's, the *Pakistani and Afghan Talibans, Saudi Al Qaeda,* the *Sunni Daëch* and other fundamentalist groups in Africa and in the Middle-East.

Alas, the Saudi and the Iranian orthodoxy founded, raised, fed, developed, and financed these terrorist organizations. Still, Iran no longer powered formations or terrorist movements after the death of Khomeini, because all Imams became responsible for the policies of the country, and all jihadist groups like the Shiite Hezbollah were turned into Lebanese defense forces. The only source of "evil", therefore, is exclusively the Sunni orthodoxy adopted by Saudi Arabia, and offered to the world through international bodies such as the Arab League, the Council of the Gulf and, the Muslim World League (MWL, located in Riyadh), which operates all over the world, especially through the Cultural Islamic Centers of every single nation. According to the Western world, the MWL is the actual international instrument of Saudi proselytism, and it represents the Saudi Puritanism-conservative perspective.

The strategic pact between the United States and Saudi Arabia was signed in 1917. The whole Arabian Peninsula came into the sphere of American influence because President Woodrow Wilson considered it a "fundamental and vital strategic location for maritime transportation"; ten years later, Saudi Arabia achieved its independence, and it became the heart of energy resources' production in the world.

Since 1927, the United States and the rest of the Western world have always given their trust to the worthless international policies adopted in the Mediterranean area by the Saudi conservative orthodoxy. This infamous and outdated pact is still running today, so new questions arise if one look at the international norms regulating Armed Conflicts in Humanitarian Law, which is the set of international rules that should ensure the respect of the fundamental human rights in the territories affected by wars. Indeed, the prohibition of torture and slavery, freedom of thought and religion, and the principle of non-discrimination fall within special international legislation that most nations, especially those involved in current conflicts, have duly signed. The violent nature of war violates the fundamental right to life, which is binding upon all states; Humanitarian Law defends this right as much as possible and at all costs, particularly through the prohibition of arbitrary executions.

The main instruments of Humanitarian Law are the four Geneva Conventions of 1949, and the two additional protocols of 1977. Almost all countries have signed these agreements, even Saudi Arabia; but, Daëch did not sign the document, and it is not a recognized state. Without examining faultfinding particulars, one have to simply recall the Geneva Convention of August 12, 1949, for the protection of civilians in time of war (the Fourth Convention). Several articles of the convention protect women, because the latter are often used as weapons of war or they are subjects of rape and violence. How many cases of rape and violence have happened in

Iraq and Syria, and nobody had the courage to denounce these crimes?

Other "grave breaches" in Humanitarian Law include the following; 1) threatening a person's life 2) *taking hostages* 3) violating human dignity 4) making use of humiliating and degrading behaviors 5) *issuing sentences and carrying out executions without a fair process*. The International Criminal Court (ICC) is responsible for punishing these crimes and others, such as crimes of genocide, crimes against humanity, and all those war crimes included and not in the Geneva conventions. The international community, non-governmental organizations (NGOs), and intergovernmental organizations (IGOs) repeatedly asked for a common regulation that could respond to these issues; and, it now seems that the international actors have found a common agreement, therefore, they recently promoted the Statute of the International Criminal Court and updated the interpretations of Humanitarian law.

Daëch has violated all these regulations, but the UN General Assembly and the Security Council have not issued any resolutions against the terrorist group. Why? Besides, the UN Human Rights Council that was created on purpose in 2006 has not taken decisions, yet. Why? Probably because the US pressed for the nomination of a Saudi Arabian in the position of President of the Council. Moreover, on the last January 2, Saudi Arabia sentenced to death many criminals and carried out their executions. Are these not violations of Humanitarian Law? Finally, should the international community fight against the Saudi orthodoxy and try to make it more reasonable, if the former must also destroy Daëch and other jihadist groups?

Chapter XIII - The Reason(s) Behind the Russian Intervention in Syria

In this chapter, answers to the previous questions will be provided. There are up to forty thousand jihadists and "foreign fighters" controlling ten provinces in Iraq, seven in Syria and three (partially) in Libya, where nearly eight million civilians live in these areas. The world can recognize the establishment of a State, as ISIS proclaimed itself on the last 19 June 2014, only if the former accepts the ideological, moral, and formal presence of the Caliphate, and the majority of the population can contribute to the economic development of the conquered provinces. Thus, ISIS is a caliphate and a State in all respects, although the international community does not recognize it. In addition, a mere terrorist group could not possibly run a State, because it requires an administration, an army, a wide perimeter, a legal structure, and an economy that can satisfy the needs of society.

In Syria, this reality was clearer than in Iraq. Initially, the armed opposition to Assad willingly accepted the presence of the Iraqi Salafis, but the two groups realized soon that they had different goals; in particular, the ELS aimed to annihilate the forces of Al Assad to restore the Sunni Syrian State, while ISIS intended to assimilate Syria under the banner of the Caliphate. In fact, in September 2015, ISIS consolidated its presence in northern Syria, while it conducted operations of infiltration from Homs to the Lebanese border on the north of Damascus; at that time, Russians did not intervene in support of the regular forces of Assad, yet. In practice, the Syrian army of Assad and the oppositions were deadlocked, while ISIS moved towards the borders of Lebanon.

Now, it is time to identify the actors who provided backup to ISIS in order to understand the reasons that encouraged the Russian intervention in Syria. ISIS sprang from Al Nousra, which used to be Al Qaeda in Iraq, and it used to receive funds from Saudi Arabia; besides, the CIA covertly supported the latter until 2012. In this moment, the Brzezinski strategy implemented by the United States in the Mediterranean and the Middle East, since 2009, received the opportunity to apply again the "permanent instability" strategy, according which a State needs to generate a valid reason(s) to implement the "proxy war" model.

Looking at the current situation from the American perspective, Russia and Iran have fallen into a trap that was set up by the US government as a direct consequence of the experience gained through the Soviet-Afghan War. In fact, there is no doubt that the CIA provided funds to ISIS (US and Saudi Arabia); as evidence shows, the Republican Senator and candidate for the White House, John McCain, had personal relations with Al Baghdadi, with all the leaders of the jihadists of Al Nousra, and with Al Qaeda in Iraq. According to Edward Snowden, found-father of WikiLeaks and responsible for the Data-gate US, there is also evidence demonstrating that the CIA provided training and armaments to ISIS. In detail, there is a document describing a secret operation codenamed "Hornets' Nest", where the target is to "protect the Jewish State by creating an enemy to its borders, but unleash it against the Islamic states who contrast its presence" (published by Snowden).

Al-Baghdadi was a prisoner at Guantanamo between 2004 and 2009. In that period, he took agreements with the CIA and the Mossad, which gave him the mandate to form a group capable of attracting and combining jihadists from several countries. He probably started to recruit in the Sunni Iraq, so to keep the Sunni away from Israel. The main goal was to create a Sunni armed front able to curb, with terrorist guerrilla actions, the Shiite dominance in Iraq; at the same time, Al-Baghdadi controlled a Sunni "army" that could be sent in support to the opposition forces to overthrow the Syrian President Bashar Al Assad! The US plan turned against itself; the strategy adopted by the American government marginally affected the creation of a Shiite State in Iraq, so that Al Qaeda (which had an agreement with the CIA) became the Islamic State, then it changed name into ISIS. The already dire situation became far more dangerous when the leaders of the new terrorist group announced that both the Shiites in Iraq and the Sunnis who refused to submit to the Caliphate were enemies of ISIS. While a

90

smokescreen covers Obama's eyesight, Putin is promptly identifying "the enemy" to annihilate it, in spite of his personal strategic interests in Syria (Obama only recently realized that Al Qaeda and Osama Bin Laden in Afghanistan had never been credible partners, but they rather acted exclusively for their own interest in terrorizing and destabilizing the world!).

The American slogan addressed to the Soviets in Afghanistan "damned if they intervene, damned if they do not intervene", confirming the "proxy war" theory, seems to have found its practical implementation in Syria, where Russia has officially sided with Assad, since last September. However, the US has forgotten about an important factor; no more than a year ago, ISIS entered into northern Iraq, it triumphed over the regular governmental troops and it killed the Shiite, Jews, Kurds, and Christians on its way. Finally freed from her responsibilities as Secretary of State, Hillary Clinton was interviewed by Jeffrey Goldberg of *The Atlantic* magazine, and she said that she had an argument with President Obama in relation to the topic "insurgents in Iraq" at the end of 2011. She claimed that,

> "It was a failure. We failed to create a credible anti-Assad insurgency. Islamists, secularists, ultra-orthodox Sunnis, and others formed it. The failure of this project provoked the horrors we are now witnessing in Iraq and Syria."

In another interview that dates back to last February, Clinton added

> "President Obama told me: 'When you have a professional army that fights against farmers, carpenters, and engineers who create riots, you must do something. Unfortunately, it is difficult to change the equation of the forces that are already on stage, but we must try.' At the time, I did not understand. Today everything is clear."

Following the words of the next Democratic candidate for the US presidency, the Russian intervention in Syria was expected and it took place at the right time. Besides, Americans have to stay away from the Middle East until the International community will announce that ISIS is not anymore harmful for the creation of a peace process that will be reached in a matter of short time, once the terrorist groups is annihilated. Unfortunately, the jihadists of ISIS have rapidly conquered new areas and they have always taken possession of the administrative power. Often, local populations tacitly helped or openly supported the terrorist group.

To liberate these areas, the West must engage the enemy by using traditional warfare methods, involving rapid street-by-street soldiers' firefights, like the Kurds in northern Iraq, in Syrian cities, and at the borders with Turkey. This is a civil war where there are no brothers fighting against each other, but the enemy is a State that goes far beyond the values that characterize the modern vision of Islamic identity and culture. In fact, ISIS focuses relentlessly on the origins of the religious character that historically belong to the Arab Caliphate.

Why the Russian army stepped into this conflict, while the others (the Saudi armed forces, Jordanian, Egyptian and so on) comfortably monitored the situation without intervening? The answer is in Ibn Rushd's treaties of Islamic philosophy (the Western world know him as Averroes); the most relevant part of his treaties is related to the separation between the temporal and the spiritual power, with the secularization of the civil State that occurred during the French and American revolutions (1700). Furthermore, Averroes is famous for his work titled *The Incoherence of philosophers' incoherence* and *Decisive Treaty*.

Therefore, why there was a Russian intervention when the international community was silent about the horrors occurring in the Middle East, and two Sunni factions tacitly reached an agreement of mutual non-aggression in Syria? Originally, ISIS used to be Al Qaeda, so the opposition armed forces of the Free Syrian Army (FSA) and the jihadists of the Qaeda worked side by side against Assad; however, the FSA realized that ISIS was going to absorb it, once the latter would become a Caliphate. Hence, these two parties found a useful pact of non-aggression after the fall of Saddam. Other Sunni groups that are interested to operate on Syrian territory, like Saudi Arabia, could apply the same approach! Due to the fact that the US government has always been an ally with Saudi

Arabia (including the dark side, which still needs to be clarified!), the Western power cannot do more than throwing bombs on the "strategic sites" of ISIS (lame and useless!).

The situation on the battlegrounds is much more complex than the systems of mass communication dare to say. In fact, multiple actors are fighting a myriad of small-scale conflicts within the major War in Syria. For instance, Shiite fight against Sunni for cultural and religious hegemony throughout the Muslim world. In addition, Saudi Arabia, Iran, and Turkey entered in conflict with one another for the supremacy in the region. Ultimately, the US, Europe, and Russia compete against each other to take permanent control of the most productive region of oil in the world, which is still a strategic priority for the West.

The UN Peace Talks that should have taken place on February 3, in Geneva, were actually postponed to the end of the month; so, the United States and the Secretary of State Kerry accused Moscow and Damascus of seeking only "the military solution" to solve the war in Syria. In reality, Russia is currently conducting an unequalled offensive in the Shiite sites of Aleppo, bombing the area and sending (as support) the ground forces of Assad and the Lebanese Hezbollah, so to free the city from ISIL. However, the latter has found support in the ex-opposition forces (FSA) who merged into rebel groups that are now controlled by terrorist organizations such as Jabhat al-Nusra and Al Qaeda; the second organization is the one from which Al Baghdadi formed the ISIS.

Due to the complexity of alliances that is typical of the Arab culture, Putin's Russia has chosen to go to war alongside with Assad and with the tacit support of Iran against ISIS. Perhaps, the real reason for the delay on the UN Peace Talks can be identified on how the United States has interpreted the current Russian campaign in Syria. Furthermore, Saudi Arabia has an ambiguous and deceitful approach against international terrorism, because 47 people received their death penalty and were executed in 2015, including the Saudi Shiite Imam Al Nimr. His murder put under the spotlight the ideological-religious conflict between Iran and Saudi Arabia, which has continued for the last 1,634 years!

The Russian intervention in Syria pointed out and clarified the fact that all forms of violence like terrorism, Jihadism, despotism, cruelty, and trivial "religious submission to the Caliph" are not tolerated, and the best resolution is the total - material and ideological - annihilation of all threats.

Although this is the best way to fight against fundamentalism, the international community have to acknowledge the difference between the Arab-Islamic and the Western cultures. This topic highlights the mistakes committed by the US in the implementation of the "permanent instability" strategy that was adopted in the recent decades. Moreover, Europe has been the great absent on the international stage, although European policies may change in the near future. Eventually, President Obama seems to have new plans in Syria, where he seems to confirm the desire to promote diplomatic talks and trade activities with Iran.

Chapter XIV - "After all, Tomorrow is Another Day". Senator Trump as an Open Window to the Future

Rossella O'Hara, in the famous film *Gone with the Wind*, utters, "After all, Tomorrow is Another Day" in her moments of great dismay. Her faithful words should "bring back" in one's mind the meaning of "hope" conceived as the belief that all matters in life can change and improve.

The life of peoples who live in the Mediterranean and the Middle East is continuously threatened by revolutions, uprisings, fratricidal wars, and civil and more conventional conflicts that cause hate, death, despair, massacres, violence, destruction, carnages, slaughters, and "sacrifices". Sunni against Shiite and vice versa, Sunni against Sunni, Muslims against Christians, fundamentalists and jihadists wildly shooting on civilians who would rather live comfortably in the culture of peaceful coexistence.

The word *God* terrifies journalists who should use it in their articles to denounce the tragedies that are occurring in the Mediterranean area and the Middle East. However, this word becomes sacred in the sick mind of murderers who sacrifice human victims for the sake of their false "god" and to re-establish an ancient religious way of life that is 1437 years old! (Hegira, the Islamic calendar). I intentionally did not write the word *god* using a capital letter because "the God of Muslims" and other monotheist religions is more merciful than the "god of ISIS" which promotes the total submission to the Caliphate.

The individual Arab belonging to the ancient era that the violent, hedonistic, and presumptuous terrorist organizations like ISIS, jihadist, and fundamentalists are trying to bring back in the Middle East, is conceived as a human being who had the privilege to be the only direct interlocutor with God (the Arab). The Arab is an isolated being that God created, but he cannot live isolated from God itself; and, he must obediently follow and respect the divine law that the *Koran of Medina* imposed on him! In light of these facts, the Arab mainly takes care of himself, even though the family is part of a more articulated social context called *the tribe,* whose members must share the same blood (blood brothers). Furthermore, according to the ancient Arab rationale, taking care of other members of the family means to have the supremacy over them and guarantee their survival. Is some occasions and according to some circumstances, if a person questions the superiority of another, or a first one doubts about the moral integrity of a second one, the former will be "offered" as a victim in the name of God.

This social plague is known by the name of "envy", which drove Cain to kill Abel in the biblical Genesis as well as in the Koran. Have you ever wondered why fundamentalists, in particular Daëch Libya, crave to raid Rome and subdue the West? Here, the feeling that drives these fanatics to conjecture the rise of an Islamic Rome is mere and sheer *envy*! The Mohammedan literature shows a Hadith in which the Prophet speaks of the Nahdha (the rebirth) as "The Advent, which coincide with the end of time, will begin with the re-appearance of Jesus (who is only a Prophet for Islamic religions) to the religious community (Umma)." This statement can be acknowledged from a theological point of view, because it is recognized by the Christian version of the Resurrection, too. However, according to radical-orthodox Sunni Imams, fundamentalists must conquer Rome because Jesus have to resurrect and find the Muslim Umma in the city that currently headquarters his Church.

Over the last few decades, the Mediterranean area and the Middle East have been characterized by a material, verbal, and ideological "violence" that accompanied the "arrogance" of all those people who have chosen a violent lifestyle. The Arab-Islamic world tends to emphasize feelings such disdain, pride, egoism, conceit, vanity, and hubris; besides, the individual tends to become arrogant because he is taught that he is a superior entity, due to the fact that God have chosen him for the purpose of Revelation.

However, *violence* and *arrogance* are a product of *ignorance*, which literally means "lack of knowledge" according to the Western interpretation. Knowledge, often mentioned by the Prophet Muhammad (from birth to death, *knowledge* is your cradle. Go to find it till you are in China), is none other than that set of notions that the human intellect transfers from generation to generation through science, philosophy, literature, theology and other subject. Furthermore, human intellect has strengthen the affirmation of human reason over theological faith, and this concept identifies the different approach that still differentiate the Islamic culture from the Western culture. Indeed, the Islamic world assigns priority to religion and religious traditions, while the Western world tends to promote human reason. A similar gap has emerged between the Northern and the Southern cultures of the Mediterranean area, specifically in relation to the "use of force" and violence, which widely varies among different countries.

In front of these events, the European Union, the European community, and the European policy were stunned, puzzled, and dazed. Instead of looking for the origins of these reactionary phenomena, Europe remained powerless and it observed without having the slightest desire to look beyond the fences imposed by its culture that glorifies modernity and capitalist hedonism.

Some European political philosophers timidly praised the wars of religion that occurred in Europe in the sixteenth century, after the Protestant Reformation and the Anglican schism. For instance, in August 1572, the French Catholics brutally killed thousands of Protestant Huguenots, and those barbarities happened due to the excessive thirst for power, which is the real reason of the conflicts taking place in the Islamic world, today, too. According to Islam, religion and the State are strictly intertwined with each other, and they cannot be separated; the majority of the Islamic nations has recognized and acknowledged this political and religious vision.

Hence, the European political and social instability is mainly caused by the evident cultural backwardness of the old continent, which knows almost nothing about the Islamic culture. At this stage, the two cultures have to put aside their differences, and they must start to communicate with each other in a peaceful manner. This is a long process, but it is the decisive next step. The equilibrium of both the Islamic and the European societies is at stake, especially because Islam is now an integral part of Europe. Eventually, Islamic, Christian, and Jews theologians must undergo the same comparison.

The whole scenario of the Mediterranean and the Middle East has always been a crossroads of cultures, races, and religions; above all, the three monotheistic religions, including Judaism, Christianity, and Islam developed in these areas, and they have always fought against one another.

Over the centuries, the "Islamic reformist thought" easily transcended in social models that have inevitably led to inter-ethnic, inter-religious, and cultural conflicts. It almost seems that the Mediterranean area, which usually is the cradle of unity and peace, has often been the main source of conflicts.

Despite the presence of a strong geostrategic negativity that, now more than ever, continues to appear in the Mediterranean area and in the Middle East, the peaceful dialogues among the opposing political parties in Tunisia have offered new opportunities and hope. Through the cultural comparison that was developed in the four years after the revolution, the new modernist reality of Islam has arisen; although its modernity does not deny the original traditions and customs, modern Islam seems to irreversibly accept the culture of Human Rights.

Daily local news report that both Europe and modern Islam wish to marginalize and incapacitate every fragment of Islamic fundamentalism. Not a day goes without the execution of arrests, incidents, and firefights sadly provoking the loss of human lives in the Tunisian hinterland, where the most radical of the new fundamentalist jihadists have been hiding for years, but Islamic fundamentalism must be "eradicated" at all costs. In the impenetrable mountain forests of Chaambi located in the Kasserine region, which is the enclave of terrorists linked to Al Qaeda in the Maghreb, the Tunisian Army Special Forces perform roundups in order to clean up permanently the area from the presence of Jihadists.

The future of Tunisia seems to improve thanks to the political and military strategies adopted against the Salafi Arab fundamentalists, and the support given by all the Muslims of good will is equally important and precious, although the latter is the less visible but definitely more challenging. Indeed, Modernists and Traditional Islamists came to a compromise, so they opened up peaceful dialogues in order to obtain better wellbeing. However, none of these achievements can end the war, because the Western world and modern Islam have to work harder together to wipe out radical Salafism, Sunni orthodoxy, ISIS and the other jihadist groups.

Yet, the Western world has good reasons to worry about the effective modernization of the democratic philosophy in the Arab countries. In April 2014, the Association ANFE Tunisia, in collaboration with the University of Tunis, has conducted a two-day international seminar on the topic "State, Religion, and Reason - A comparison of different cultures", with great participation from the academic society and young Tunisian students and workers. The Italian speakers (4) identified the "differences" of the two Judicial Systems as they talked about the Right of Family. Students detected these differences and they acquired the necessary "knowledge" that will set them up on the right path of "intercultural dialogue", aiming to improve social integration. As a worthy note to be mentioned, it is not enough to live in another country to assimilate the values of freedom and respect that should be the foundations of coexistence.

The general state of affairs in the Mediterranean demonstrates that there is an increasing need to study, analyze, and understand the traditions of "other cultures", so to fight back all forms of fundamentalism. On the one hand lies the "violence" that manifests itself in various ways (bestiality, racism, subjugation, ISIS and Salafis, and discrimination / intolerance / nationalist tendencies spreading around the European nations); on the other hand, although "religion" is conceived as a discriminating factor typical of Islamic nations, it is becoming an important element to build a peaceful dialogue between modernism and orthodoxy. In practice, radical Islamism acknowledges only the society that was founded by the Prophet, and this type of society is progressively reacting to the process of modernization that is occurring in many Mediterranean countries, nowadays. In detail, the jihadist fundamentalism, which took inspiration from Salafism, is a counter-reaction to the needs of the modern civil society. Fundamentalism is a manifestation of desperation that finds its strength through the sadness of oppressed and not integrated individuals.

It is for all the reasons listed in the previous paragraph that the West has the duty to encourage the exchange of "intercultural relations"; the countries of the southern Mediterranean demanded for peaceful talks. The possibility to create a dialogue and develop a common learning path with the Islamic community must stimulate the European countries to achieve greater goals, especially in this dramatic period in which refugees are flooding the coasts of Europe and Italy. The Western world is trying to protect humanity, and the dignity of these poor peoples, regardless of the cultural and racial differences.

"Humanism" is the keyword to build a better future for our grandchildren; the importance of the human being, his dignity, and his prerogatives, must be promoted so as it was so wisely expounded in the *UN Declaration of Human Rights*, in 1948. This quotation reminds that the Western world is very different from the Islamic world, although both societies need to promote intercultural exchanges. After the events that occurred in the last few months, including the rising number of migrants and the ignoble terroristic actions of ISIS, Europe must promote cultural confrontation and exchanges without exacerbating cultural differences.

The process of civilization belonging to Western nations started from the late Middle Ages, through the evaluation and review - even philosophical - of the human being and of his intellect, resulting in the development of the modern democratic systems that respect individual freedom; these systems are better known as *Societies of Rights*. On the contrary, the Islamic world is still strictly interconnected to the Will of God, and Muslims must respect the rules dictated by the Koran and the Hadith; this is the *Society of Duties*!

The outcome of the comparison between these two different *societies* is that the dominant European culture evolved in seven hundred years, and no one wishes to give it up (including European Muslims!). This evolution began with the periods of Humanism and Enlightenment, passing through the French and the American revolutions and the affirmation of democracy, then finally confirmed the centrality of human beings, their dignity and freedom; in particular, Europe respects Human Rights and the culture of the contemporary society.

Regardless of their considerable differences, all Muslim religious beliefs are based on the same sacred manuscript: the Koran. Islam is one, and it recognizes itself and its priorities in the Koranic Revelation. Islam was founded in 674 (release of the first edition of the Koran), and the sacred texts called Suras (114) do not follow a chronological order, but they are methodically organized according to their length. In particular, even though each sacred text unveils its place of origins, there is not a distinction between the Suras revealed in Mecca (610-622 AD) and those ones in Medina (622-632 AD), which gave rise to the Mecca's Islam and Medinas' Islam.

While the Mecca Suras contain universal values, the Medina Suras gave a legal, political, and social structure to the Umma. Indeed, the former correspond to the beginning of the Koranic Revelation and they were "dictated" to the Prophet himself who did not own the knowledge to educate the community, yet. The latter are less concerned with Islamic eschatology and the promotion of its values.

Besides, the international community should still remember what occurred to Pope Benedict XVI, when he questioned some verses of the Medina Suras glorifying violence in his *Lectio Magistalis* in Bratislava (2006). Furthermore, no one should forget what happened to one of the most famous Islamic theologians, Mohammed Taha, who once claimed "the Medina Suras are mostly concerned with 'politics', but they correspond to the mental, social and psychological frameworks of an Islam that belonged to the seventh century". Successively, Taha added that probably *"the prophet Mohammed, who never saw the final version of the Koran, would not include the Medina Suras in the Koran, but in another text."* As a direct consequence for asserting his statements, the theologian was condemned to death for apostasy by the Sudanese regime, which hanged him in 1985.

Once again, Islamic orthodoxy attempts to impose itself over the modernist interpretation of the manuscript. Still, through the act of *reasoned* sacrifice, Taha has outlined the path towards a more modern Islam for the future Muslim generations, eliminating all contradiction between the ancient *Will of God* and the present *civilization of Human rights*.

Taha's thoughts are more contemporary now than ever, especially in Europe where governments encourage the diffusion of human rights; by contrast, the Medina Koran subtly causes social instability and immoral behaviors. For instance, just more than a year ago, the legal English system introduced the *inheritance norm* (only for Muslims who request it) extracted from the Koran, according which women are less worth than men are. Specifically, the rule of succession establishes that Mothers can receive 1/8 of the heritage, and sons inherit double the amount of their sisters' heirloom!

As the outcome of the case in England, the Muslim world in Europe needs to urgently, peacefully, and without prejudice debate about the possible adaption of Islam to the needs of the European Civil Society, and the review of the practical religious aspects. For example, the EU and the European Islamic community should advise the Imams to place particular emphasis in saying that the Medina Suras promote social values and teachings that were valid at the time of revelation,1437 years ago (Islamic theology should confirm it!). Therefore, these social values and teachings may not be applicable to the Umma, nowadays, because Muslims willingly live in EU countries that promotes "Human Rights", and they have to comply with the laws of governments. In particular, the Ministry of Interior should call all Imams for a meeting and demand them to comply with the laws of the State on Human Rights, which must be conceived as a priority over the teachings of the Medina Koran.

Essentially, European countries need to establish a peaceful dialogue and an intercultural exchange with the entire Muslim population who live in their own territories. Moreover, they have to identify the consequences to the potential return of the Koran and Mecca Islam, and actualize the Medina Koran in full respect of human rights, which are enshrined in the will of peoples since 1948. The Muslim European citizens adhered to the Human Rights System when they willingly came to live in the old continent.

Contemporary history shows that all the attempts to promote multiculturalism in the area influenced by Western powers have failed miserably, and they actually radicalized Islam, which tends to maintain its cultural identity and to impose itself over other religions. For example, the processes of integration regarding Muslim communities in France have always been conducted according to the ancient "Jacobin" mentality, therefore, the local government asked to high-level Muslim interlocutors to sign the documents where they had to recognize the principles of republican equality, secularism, separation of church and state, and other clauses. However, the French government did not take into account that Islam, particularly the Sunni, is a "do it yourself" religion in which the self-proclaimed Sunni Imams can encourage the burst of violence and radicalization of Islam, if they claim that the content of the Medina Suras is still applicable today. Because of the erroneous French policy, ISIS has declared war against France, and the local government hunts down fundamentalists who live in the peripheral area of Paris.

In a second case, Holland unsuccessfully tried to implement a plan characterized by a pluralism of social facilities that were made available for different cultural identities. These facilities aimed to encourage intercultural dialogue between Protestants and Catholics (which today are almost unified), and excluded Muslim communities, who usually tend to impose their fundamental and untouchable model, without considering the social traditions of other cultures.

In another case, the faulty Belgian and Spanish solutions were based on social consent, but they promoted agreements constraining the freedoms of the Islamic community. Additionally, these treaties became more complicated and unsatisfying because Muslims lacked a unified theological and organizational center. For instance, all possibilities of an agreement were rendered useless because of the differences generated among the (alleged) representatives of the Muslim community in Italy, when Maroni was the Minister of Interior.

In the last case, Muslims represents nearly 2% of the American and Canadian populations, and the US has almost pushed all Muslims to the edge of society. In fact, intolerance toward Islam has reached a critical stage in the US, in spite of the strong influence that the *Council on American-Islamic Relations* (CAIR) has on President Obama and on the major representatives of the US Democratic Party. The problem is that Americans mostly perceive Muslims as potential terrorists, and rather many Shiite of Iranian origins became agnostic; this cultural shift surely accelerated social integration, but Muslims had to move away from their religious belief. Moreover, Islamic Sunni were "ghettoized" (or, perhaps, they did it according to their will) to promote interfaith coexistence through the full acceptance of the American constitutional principles; however, this process of assimilation furtherly stressed the differences among the Muslim communities.

Within this framework, the Republican Senator Donald Trump, encouraged by his supporters and fund-raisers, made himself the voice of the entire American population and he claimed *"we should block the entry of Muslims in the United States to think about the future negative consequences of integration"*. Then, he added in a speech delivered in South Carolina that the US should consider the idea of *"closing internet and social media"* to drastically reduce all forms of extremism online. Trump manifested his thoughts by using harsh words, indeed, which bring back memories of the "Red Scare" and the policy adopted by the McCarthyism in the United States. Today, the US has an extremely radicalized "political" vision of Islam, perhaps, because the population feel betrayed by the policies implemented by the current American administration.

Conclusion

No one is questioning the legitimacy of Islam as a religion and a set of religious practices, but institutions have to check on the validity of the dubious political dimension of Islam that is increasingly spreading all over the world. Once again, the case of Tunisia provides good evidence to analyze the situation in the Mediterranean Area. Within the Islamist Nahdha party, the leader Ghannuchi has long insisted to separate the "religious" thought from the political party; actually, he was the first person in his party to realize that the Islamic theocratic ideology must be isolated from the Tunisian political context that, by contrast, fully promotes Governmental Laws! This particular philosophy, if rightly applied by the American administration, could stop the Islamic threat so as the American Government had already stopped the threat of Communism in the last century. In this way, the US still have a chance to protect its Democracy and Freedom!

This phenomenon is less evident in Canada, although there is a high percentage of Pakistani immigrants in the total Canadian population (this western country is the cradle of Salafi Wahhabism!), because integration policies favor – among other things - agnosticism, the formation of a career, harmonious coexistence, critical thinking, and reason; in other words, Canada does not really promote religious policies. Examples like Canada give new hope, and let us all believe in the rise of a better Western World where human beings, in spite of their religious beliefs, are protected by the Declaration on Human Rights. This document is extremely valuable because it was written in the blood of all those who died due to inequality, oppression, holocaust, marginalization, discrimination, racism, segregation, intolerance, anti-Semitism, xenophobia, war, injustice and all other horrors that deny the protection of the fundamental "human rights".

It is for all these reasons that *Europe and the United States* must take the lead of this internal Cultural Revolution! As the Tunisian modernist culture has called to his responsibilities the orthodoxy of the Zituna Koranic School, the *Cultural and*

*Intercultural Commissions of **the Council of Europe*** and the ***Congress Commission of the United States*** have to promote Intercultural Dialogue. The main goals of these international organisms include the *"Protection of Human Rights and the primacy of Law"* on their territory, and the *"development of a national identity* (embedding Islamic values, too) *based on shared values that transcend cultural differences"*.

Policy makers have to take important cultural and political decisions that may change the several different legal aspects influencing the relationship between faith and politics, including the Constitutional Law of the EU, International Law, and the regulations on Armed Conflicts. Therefore, it is necessary to achieve a better understanding of the "Other" (Islam) through intercultural exchange and dialogue, so to find a shared sense of social life, particularly in Europe, where we have to begin walking the path of peace and unity to which we are all called.

www.ingramcontent.com/pod-product-compliance
Lightning Source LLC
Chambersburg PA
CBHW050405290526
45786CB00003B/1140